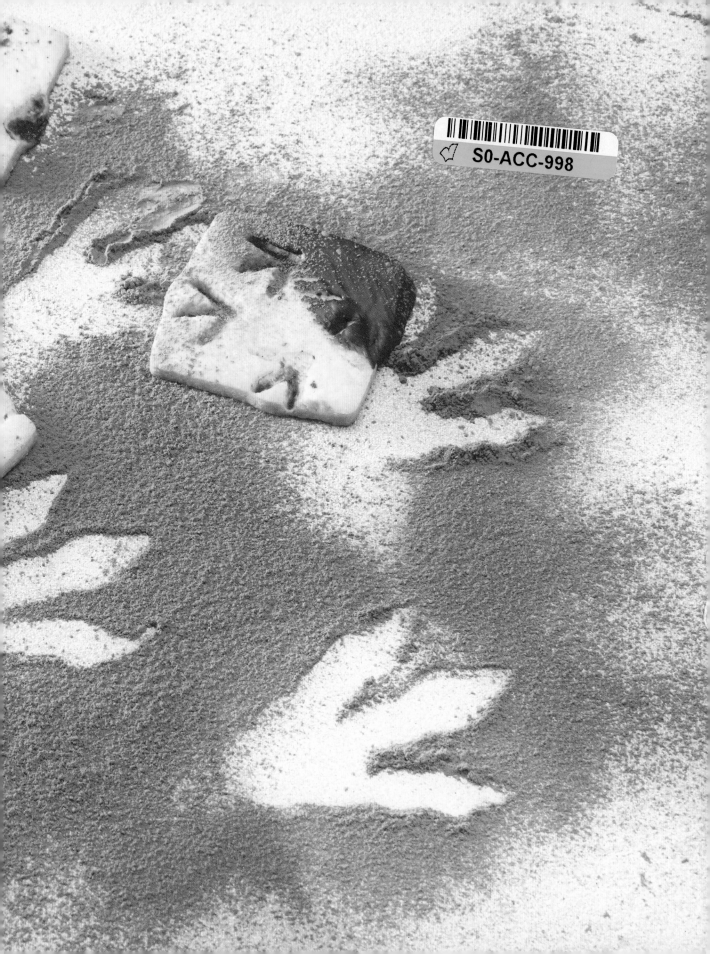

THE OFFICIAL COOKBOOK

Isla Nublar Floating Cheesecakes (Page 138)

THE OFFICIAL COOKBOOK

OVER 50 MOUTHWATERING RECIPES FROM ISLA NUBLAR

Written by **Dayton Ward**

Recipes by **Elena P. Craig**

Photography by **Ted Thomas**

INSIGHT
EDITIONS

San Rafael · Los Angeles · London

CONTENTS

63

The Splash Zone

121
Mount Sibo Volcanic Cupcakes

27
"Armored" Artichoke Plates

INTRODUCTION

Jurassic World is like no place else on Earth.

A premier theme park and all-inclusive resort, Jurassic World boasts an array of attractions and amenities unrivaled by any other vacation destination on the planet. When it comes to providing an unparalleled visitor experience, we spare no effort or expense. Every member of our team works toward the common goal of ensuring that a guest's every moment is filled with wonder and delight—whether that moment involves taking in the thrilling sights of the park or sitting down to a delicious and satisfying meal.

The world-class chefs in our restaurants, cafés, and nightclubs work tirelessly to provide delicacies to satisfy any palate, whether you're looking for fine dining, a quick snack, or a relaxing drink after a full day of adventure. You'll find a host of options designed to evoke not just a connection to the park and the wonders you'll encounter here, but also to the paradise we're privileged to call home.

As our creative and varied menu seems to enhance the experience of a visit to the park, it's only fair that guests be able to take a taste of Jurassic World home with them as they would any treasured souvenir. It is therefore with great pride and enthusiasm that we offer you the book you now hold in your hands: *Jurassic World: The Official Cookbook*, a collection of recipes for some of our chefs' most popular—and our guests' most requested—dishes and drinks.

The chapters in this cookbook are based on the spectacular, dinosaur-filled "zones" in the park, each of which showcases a different kind of dinosaur and the cuisine they've inspired. Are you cooking for big meat eaters? Flip over to Carnivore Country to discover tasty treats from T. Rex Kingdom. Looking for something leafy and green? Our chapter featuring vegetarian and vegan plates is full of plant-based eats for herbivores inspired by *Gallimimus*, *Brachiosaurus*, and some of our other gentle giants. Long after your vacation ends and you've left our island paradise, you'll be able to re-create some of the culinary creations you enjoyed during your stay with us. We hope you're hungry!

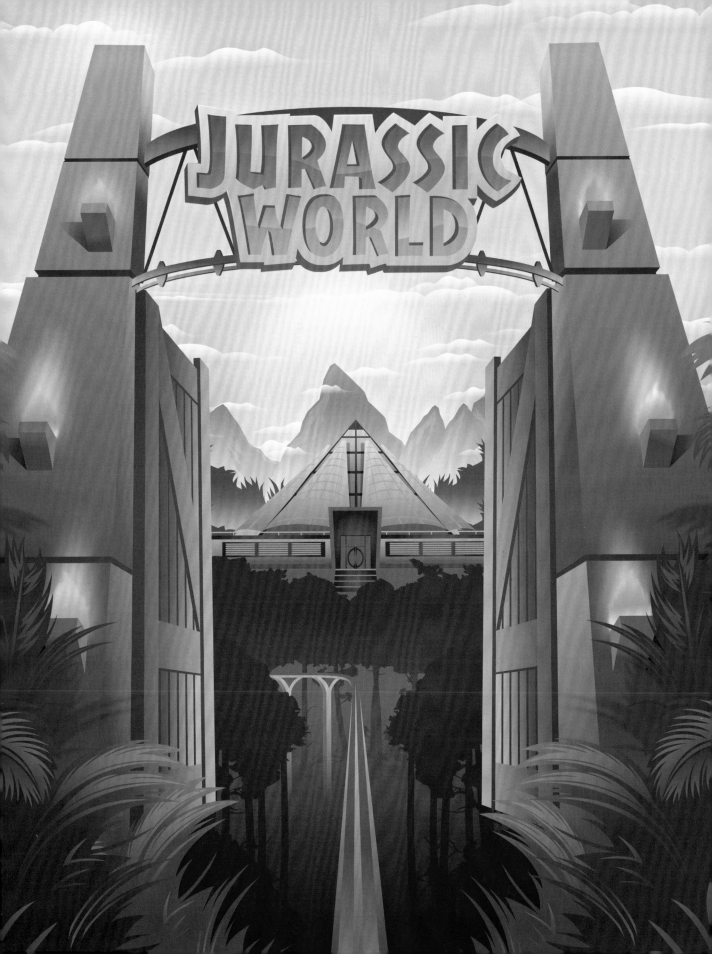

JURASSIC WORLD: FROM DREAM TO REALITY

It began as one man's singular vision.

John Hammond, keen businessman, noted philanthropist, and passionate supporter of scientific research, had nurtured from a very early age a fascination with wildlife parks and other venues that allowed people to observe animals in a safe environment. Following a successful business career, he became fascinated with the idea of cloning dinosaurs using fossilized DNA that had been preserved in substances like amber. His enthusiasm for this idea led him to partner with his longtime friend Benjamin Lockwood, and together they founded a new company, International Genetics Technologies, or "InGen." At the same time, his fundraising organization, the Hammond Foundation, continued to lend financial support to numerous paleontological excursions around the world searching for viable dinosaur DNA samples. It was through the foundation's efforts that Hammond's initial team of genetic engineers successfully cloned their first dinosaur in the mid-1980s.

Now armed with a viable specimen and the technology to reproduce the results, Hammond's next goal was to build an attraction that might showcase these new creations. While his original intention was to build an attraction in San Diego, California, he and Lockwood abandoned that idea in favor of a larger, much grander plan: a private island to serve as a self-sustaining habitat for a thriving population of cloned dinosaurs. Here, in this preserve far away from the bustle of human civilization, animals that had not walked the Earth for millions of years would once again roam free . . . under careful care and observation, of course. However, the park would not just serve as an attraction for throngs of dinosaur-loving guests; it would also act as a working laboratory and a state-of-the-art research and development facility.

Initial efforts to bring "Jurassic Park" to life were met with numerous challenges and obstacles. Amid rising doubts over the premise's profitability, Hammond eventually left InGen and retired, choosing to direct his efforts toward environmental activism. In 1998, a year after Hammond's death, InGen was purchased by the Masrani Corporation. The Masrani Corporation's founder, Simon Masrani, firmly believed that Hammond's dream of a "dinosaur park open to the public" could be realized. Beginning in 2002, he put his audacious plan into action, funneling much-needed capital into InGen to ramp up its genetic engineering efforts. At the same time, Masrani put into motion the development and construction of an unparalleled new attraction on Isla Nublar: Jurassic World (off the coast of Costa Rica).

Since opening in 2005, Jurassic World has attracted nearly 100,000 visitors each month. Far more than a simple zoo for dinosaurs, it is the park Hammond originally imagined: a thriving ecosystem representing a time on Earth once believed to be lost to the ages. It provides an unprecedented opportunity to learn about the past and how it informs our present—and perhaps even how it guides us toward our future. Everything we do here is born from the dream of one man, John Hammond, in service to all the people of Earth. For in order to best prepare for where we wish to go, we must first understand from where we came.

Welcome . . . to Jurassic World!

A GLOSSARY OF COMMON TERMS, TOOLS, AND TECHNIQUES

Below is a brief overview of some of the tools, techniques, and ingredients used in this cookbook.

Tools:

BAKING MAT

A nonstick reusable baking sheet made of high-quality food-grade silicone which lays flat in the bottom of a baking pan or tray. Baking mats come in a variety of sizes and are often used in place of parchment paper when the food is especially hot or sticky. This is listed as a Special Supply for the Amber Lollipops (page 103).

CELLOPHANE TREAT BAGS

Small clear plastic bags used to hold candy or wrap other treats. These are a Special Supply for the Amber Lollipops (page 103) and the Popcorn Tail Clubs (page 106).

COOKIE CUTTERS

Used to neatly cut cookies or candies into defined shapes. A square one is recommended for the Dino Tracks Shortbread Cookies (page 118) and a flower-shaped one for the Coconut Fudge (page 88).

COOKIE SCOOP

When a recipe calls for a cookie scoop, it's referring specifically to a scoop that has a rotating piece of metal that scrapes the dough out of the scoop when you squeeze the handle. It is a good idea to have a few of these on hand in a variety of sizes; they're extremely useful for portioning out any number of things: dough, batter, ice cream, and any kind of wet, sticky mixture.

DUTCH OVEN

A large heavy cooking pot usually made of cast iron. This can go on the stove or in the oven and is great at retaining heat, making it the perfect cooking vessel for just about everything.

FOOD PROCESSOR

An electronic kitchen tool that consists of a plastic bowl fitted over a set of spinning blades, which can be used to assist in a variety of food prep, including chopping, shredding, pulverizing, mixing, and more. Usually comes with at least two speeds and a pulse option to create short bursts of processing. More commonly (but not exclusively) used to prep dry ingredients before cooking.

FRY THERMOMETER

A frying thermometer helps you measure the temperature of oils in recipes where precise temperatures are critical. A candy thermometer works in the same way. A fry thermometer is made of thick glass that can handle the heat and often has a clip on the side that you can attach to your pot so you don't have to hold it while you are waiting for your oil to reach the appropriate temperature.

JUMBO CUPCAKE PAN

This is a pan that usually makes 6 muffins or cupcakes rather than 12. Each cake will measure 2.5 inches across the bottom.

KITCHEN SHEARS

Kitchen shears are scissors made specifically for food preparation. These come with a variety of features depending on how fancy you want to get. However, the key feature that all kitchen shears should have is their ability to come apart. The blades should separate so they can be cleaned individually. Using normal craft scissors in the kitchen is unhygienic and not recommended.

MANDOLINE

A mandoline slicer is a kitchen tool that is used to slice vegetables, potatoes, and other foods very thinly. Most mandolines have a handgrip, a finger guard, a flat angled surface like a slide, and a very sharp blade. You use it by dragging a vegetable downward against the blade away from you. Some of them are fairly simple with one thickness setting while others have multiple settings and various attachments. However, amateur chefs should be warned: Mandolines have a reputation for being dangerous. They work because the blade is extremely sharp and even professional chefs have been known to wear wire-mesh gloves when using them. Be cautious and never use one when children are present. Thicker veggie slices are better than sliced fingers!

PASTRY BAGS & TIPS

A pastry bag is a cone-shaped bag which is usually used to pipe frosting or icing on cakes, cookies, cupcakes, and other desserts. These come in disposable and reusable options and usually come with a set of attachable tips to create different shapes in your frosting. Some disposable options are microwave-safe, which is useful for melting chocolate or other items (be sure to check the packaging before trying this). Aside from decorating desserts, they can also be used to pipe batter, dough, creams, or pureed ingredients ahead of cooking.

PASTRY CUTTER

A pastry cutter or pastry blender is a handheld baking tool made of several U-shaped wires attached to a sturdy wood or metal handle. It is used to cut cold butter into flour for pastries, scones, and other baked goods where a light, flaky, or crumbly texture is desired. If you don't have a pastry cutter on hand, you can use two forks to break up the butter, cutting it into the flour. Hold one fork in each hand, and pull them in opposite directions. Either of these methods will incorporate the small pieces of butter into the flour, rather than dissolving the butter, and the mixture will have a coarse, crumbly texture.

Techniques:

CHIFFONADE

A chiffonade is a slicing technique for turning leafy green vegetables such as kale and flat herbs such as basil into long, thin ribbons. To do this, stack the leaves on top of each other, and roll them tightly together. Then slice the leaves thinly, perpendicular to the roll.

CROSS-HATCHING

Cross-hatching is a type of scoring pattern in meat that creates an attractive cross pattern on the surface and exposes more surface area to heat, resulting in more even cooking. To create the pattern, use a very sharp knife and create a series of diagonal slashes going in one direction across the surface of the meat. Do not let your knife penetrate deeper than 1/8 to 1/4 of an inch. Repeat this process with the slashes going in the opposite direction across the first set.

CRUMB COAT

A preliminary very thin layer of frosting used to "glue" any crumbs down and provide an even base for the decorative layer of frosting.

DEGLAZE

Deglazing is a technique for getting caramelized bits of food up from the bottom of a pan to incorporate into a sauce. This is done by simply adding liquid to the hot pan—the caramelized bits should detach from the bottom immediately or with some light scraping with a wooden spoon. This not only adds an enjoyable depth of flavor to sauces and final dishes, but it aids in cleanup as well.

FLOAT

When making layered cocktails, you use the weight of each ingredient and the method of slowly pouring each over the back of a spoon to "float" each layer on top of the last. The spoon should be held just above the surface of the liquid in the glass and ideally braced against the side of the glass.

DEEP-FRYING

Deep-frying is very convenient in a deep-fryer, however you can still do it even if you don't have one. To set up your deep-fry station, place a Dutch oven or large, deep, heavy-bottom pan on the burner. Attach a fry thermometer to the side of the pan, and fill it with an oil of your choice, enough to submerge your food. Some common types of oil used for frying are canola, safflower, and peanut oil (olive oil is not recommended due to its lower smoke point and strong flavor, which can transfer to your food). Bring the oil slowly up to the temperature specified in the recipe. You will need to monitor and possibly adjust the heat throughout cooking, as adding food to the oil will cause the temperature to drop. When the oil has come up to temperature, you are ready to deep-fry.

When deep-frying, please observe the following safety guidelines. Keep your station tidy and clear of any unnecessary utensils, ingredients, or other items. Before you add food to oil, use a paper towel to remove as much moisture as possible. Never add water to hot oil; it will splash and bubble and could result in oil escaping the pan. Never drop the food in the oil. Instead, place it gently in the pan using metal tongs, and wear protective cooking mitts, if necessary. Do not touch oil with your bare skin or place your hand inside the Dutch oven or pan. Monitor your thermometer closely, and do not let the heat get too high. If the oil gets too hot it will start to smoke and could catch fire. Always have a lid nearby to cover the pan in the event of fire. Never leave your deep-fry station unattended. Additionally, it is not advised to let children assist with deep-frying or get too close to the deep-fry station.

PAN TOASTING

Toasting nuts causes them to release their essential oils, making them more fragrant and flavorful. To toast them in a pan, place a dry skillet over medium-high heat. Once the pan is hot, add nuts in a single layer and cook, stirring occasionally, for 1 minute. Remove the pan from the heat, and continue to toast 2 to 3 minutes more, stirring once or twice (this will help to keep them from burning). Remove nuts from the pan when fragrant.

STEMMING KALE

Slice the leaf of the kale away from the stem by running a sharp chef's knife against the length of the stalk on both sides.

Ingredients:

BUTTER

All recipes in this book call for salted butter unless otherwise specified.

COCONUT MILK

Coconut milk comes in several varieties—the most common being full fat and lite. When working with the full fat, unless otherwise instructed, make sure to thoroughly blend it, either by shaking the can or decanting it into a bowl and whisking.

FLOUR

There are as many types of flour as there are types of dinosaurs, and which kind you use depends largely on what you're trying to make. Then again, there are times, such as when it's being used as a thickener or binding agent, when it doesn't matter as much. For those recipes when it does matter, we have specified the type of flour in the ingredients list (i.e., all-purpose, self-raising). For those recipes where it doesn't matter, you are free to use whatever you have on hand.

LUSTER DUST

A food-safe glitter that can be purchased online or in specialty baking departments. It can be mixed with clear alcohol to create a shimmery paint or brushed on dry.

SALTS

There are certain recipes in this book where a specific salt is called out, such as kosher, sea, or lava. If it is not specified, table salt or your salt of choice is fine. Kosher salt is sometimes called for in baking because it is additive free and disperses easily. Sea salt is a great finishing salt and works well with things that aren't going to cook for a long time. The lava salt suggested in the Coconut Fudge recipe (page 88) is used for its unique taste and color.

Vegetarian and vegan dishes from Gyrosphere Valley and beyond

The Gyrosphere Valley region of Jurassic World is devoted to the island's large herds of (mostly) peaceful leaf-eating dinosaurs and offers amazing opportunities to get especially close to our herds of *Triceratops* and *Gallimimus*. Guests can take a ride in one of our exclusive Gyrospheres and see these gentle creatures up close, along with dinosaurs from other families of herbivores such as *Pachyrhinosaurus*, *Sinoceratops*, and *Stegosaurus*. The plants and fruits growing wild on the island are in particular abundance in this area, satisfying our dinosaurs' nutritional needs as well as providing inspiration for the vegetarian and vegan dishes you'll find in the park—and in this chapter. Here, we've collected recipes for several of our chefs' favorite dishes, which are sure to bring back memories of your visit to Jurassic World and Gyrosphere Valley in particular.

DINOSAUR KALE SALAD

Kale is one of the most versatile greens, equally delicious when served raw or cooked. For this delectable, healthy salad, use dino kale (also called Tuscan kale) as the base; add a selection of nuts and seeds; and serve with vinaigrette dressing. It's the perfect lunch for happy, healthy herbivores everywhere.

YIELD: 4 SERVINGS

1 large bunch dinosaur kale, stemmed, washed, and dried

8 tablespoons olive oil, divided

½ teaspoon kosher salt, divided

¼ cup apple cider vinegar

2 teaspoons molasses

Juice of half a lime

½ cup roasted, unsalted, shelled pistachios

½ cup shaved Parmesan (about 2 ounces)

½ cup pomegranate arils (seeds)

1. Cut the kale into ribbons by loosely rolling the leaves and slicing them into thin strips (this is called a large-scale chiffonade). Place the kale ribbons in a serving bowl. Pour 2 tablespoons of the olive oil and ¼ teaspoon of the salt over the kale, and massage it gently with your hands, making sure that all the ribbons are coated. Set aside.

2. In a small bowl, combine the remaining 6 tablespoons of olive oil, remaining ¼ teaspoon of salt, vinegar, molasses, and lime juice. Whisk thoroughly until emulsified. Pour the dressing over the kale, and toss to coat. If you have extra dressing left over, which is likely, pour it into a mason jar and store in the refrigerator for up to 4 days.

3. Toss in the pistachios, cheese, and pomegranate seeds, and serve.

TIP:

After tossing the kale with the dressing, the salad can rest up to a half hour, at room temp, before serving. It can also be refrigerated for up to 3 hours.

ROOT VEGETABLE CHIPS

The baked chips served at Jurassic World are created from root vegetables such as carrots, yams, beets, and turnips. They offer a healthier and more flavorful alternative to fried potato chips and are a popular, energizing snack or side for many park visitors.

YIELD: 4 TO 6 SERVINGS

2 pounds of a selection of root vegetables, such as potatoes, beets, rutabaga, carrots, parsnips, yams, or sweet potatoes
2 to 3 tablespoons sea salt
¼ cup olive oil

SPECIAL SUPPLIES:
Mandolin
Pastry brush

TIP:
Veggie chips will continue to crisp as they cool.

1. Scrub the vegetables clean, and peel as desired. Carefully use a mandolin to slice all the vegetables paper-thin, and then spread them out on a paper towel. Sprinkle with sea salt, and let rest for 15 minutes.
2. Preheat the oven to 300°F. Prepare two baking sheets or cookie sheets by lining them with parchment paper and brushing them with a thin layer of olive oil.
3. Blot any moisture off the surface of the vegetables, and arrange them on the parchment-lined baking sheets so that they're touching but not overlapping. Brush tops very lightly with oil (the underside will pick up oil from the parchment). Bake for 15 minutes, then rotate the racks, removing any vegetables that have already browned and crisped, and bake an additional 10 to 15 minutes or until remaining vegetables are brown and mostly crispy (the chips will continue to crisp as they cool). Allow to cool completely before serving, or store them in an airtight container for 3 to 4 days.

SERVED WITH VOLCANIC HUMMUS (PAGE 20)

VOLCANIC HUMMUS

Lending itself to countless variations, hummus is a popular addition to any spread. While our recipe isn't nearly as hot as the lava that might have once come pouring out of Isla Nublar's Mount Sibo, this combination of red and black lentil hummuses has a bold, spicy flavor and creamy consistency that makes it a wonderful companion to many of the dishes you'll find in this book.

YIELD: APPROXIMATELY 2 CUPS OF EACH DIP

FOR THE RED LENTIL HUMMUS:

1½ cups water
½ tablespoon vegetable bouillon paste
½ cup red lentils
1 bay leaf
2 cloves garlic, peeled
¼ cup roasted red pepper, diced
2 tablespoons tahini
1 teaspoon paprika
Juice and zest of ½ a lemon
Pinch of sea salt, to taste

FOR THE BLACK LENTIL HUMMUS:

1½ cups water
½ tablespoon vegetable bouillon paste
½ cup beluga or black lentils
Pinch of red pepper flakes, to taste
1 tablespoon toasted sesame seeds
2 tablespoons tahini
1 tablespoon olive oil
½ teaspoon paprika
Juice of ½ lemon
¼ teaspoon cumin

1 package pita bread, to serve
Paprika, to serve
Olive oil, to serve

TO MAKE THE RED LENTIL HUMMUS:

1. Combine the water, bouillon paste, lentils, and bay leaf in a small saucepan over medium heat. Bring to a boil, cover, and then reduce to a simmer for 10 to 12 minutes, until most of the liquid is gone. Uncover, stir, and cook another 2 to 3 minutes. When the lentils are creamy, transfer to a small bowl, cover, and let cool for about 20 minutes. Remove bay leaf.
2. In the bowl of a food processor, pulse the garlic until finely chopped, then add red peppers, tahini, paprika, lemon juice and zest, and a pinch of salt. Pulse until combined. Scrape down the sides of the bowl, add the cooled lentils, and pulse until smooth.

TO MAKE THE BLACK LENTIL HUMMUS:

3. Combine the water, bouillon paste, lentils, and red pepper flakes in a small saucepan over medium heat. Bring to a boil, cover, and then reduce to a simmer for 20 minutes. Uncover, then simmer for 15 to 20 minutes more, until the lentils are tender and most of the liquid is gone. Transfer lentils to a small bowl, cover, and let cool for about 20 minutes.
4. Add the cooled lentils to the bowl of a food processer along with the rest of the ingredients, and pulse until combined and mostly smooth.

TO SERVE:

5. Preheat the oven to 375°F.
6. Cut the pita bread into triangles. Brush each piece with olive oil, place on a baking sheet, and toast in an oven for 5 to 8 minutes, or until golden brown.
7. Scoop the dips side by side into a large shallow bowl. Sprinkle the paprika on the red dip, and drizzle olive oil on the black dip. Arrange the pita around the dips.

IGUANODON AVOCADO PESTO

Avocados have been around for more than ten thousand years, but it is safe to assume that they would have been a hit among herbivores like *Iguanodon* had they been around when it roamed the earth 126 million years ago! Here they form the base for a flavorful pesto that makes a smooth, silky topping for pasta or rice. We recommend serving with Shrimp à la Isla Nublar (page 59)

YIELD: 4 TO 6 SERVINGS

4 cloves garlic
⅓ cup pine nuts, toasted
1 big bunch of cilantro leaves
1½ cups grated Parmesan cheese
Juice of 1 lime
½ teaspoon salt
Fresh ground black pepper, to taste
1 ripe avocado
½ cup olive oil

TO SERVE:
1 pound pasta or 4 cups cooked rice

TO MAKE THE PESTO:

1. Add the first four ingredients to a food processor one at a time and process, stopping after each ingredient to scrape down the sides of the bowl. Add the lime, salt, and black pepper to taste. Add the avocado, and puree until mostly smooth.
2. With the food processor running, slowly add up to ½ cup of olive oil until mixture reaches a thick mayonnaise consistency. Set aside.

TO SERVE:

3. Cook pasta or rice according to package directions. Toss pasta or rice with pesto while still hot, and serve immediately.

FIELD NOTES:

Iguanodon often travel in herds, making it harder for a predator to pick one out of a group.

JURASSIC FRITTERS

A tantalizing snack for human herbivores, this South American-inspired fritter gets a ton of flavor from green onion, rice wine vinegar, and Monterey Jack cheese. In the park, we often serve this treat with our Volcanic Hummus (page 20) and we recommend you do the same.

YIELD: ABOUT 20 PATTIES

Two 15-ounce cans black beans, drained and rinsed, divided

1 tablespoon rice wine vinegar

½ tablespoon kosher salt

½ cup all-purpose flour

½ teaspoon baking powder

1 egg

½ cup finely grated Monterey Jack cheese

⅓ cup roughly chopped parsley leaves

⅓ cup green onions, white and light green parts, thinly sliced (about 4 to 5 onions)

About 1 cup oil for frying, such as corn or safflower

SPECIAL SUPPLIES:

1½-inch cookie scoop

Fry thermometer

1. Add 2 cups of the black beans to the bowl of a food processor, along with the vinegar and salt. Blend until mostly smooth. Add the flour and baking powder, and continue to blend until incorporated, scraping down sides as needed. Add the egg, and process until incorporated. At this point, the mixture should resemble a dough. Add the cheese, remaining black beans, parsley, and green onion, pulsing once or twice after each addition, until just combined. Transfer the black bean mixture to the refrigerator, and chill for at least 30 minutes.

2. Line a large plate with paper towel. In a medium-size high-sided skillet fitted with a fry thermometer, heat ¼ inch of oil to 350°F. Using the cookie scoop, carefully scoop a ball of the black bean mixture into the hot oil and allow it to fry for about 30 seconds before flipping with a wide spatula and smashing flat, to about a ¼-inch thick. Brown 1 to 2 minutes more on each side until a deep golden brown. Remove from oil and let drain on a paper towel-lined plate or baking sheet. Repeat until all the black bean mixture is gone.

3. Serve with the Volcanic Hummus dip (page 20) and warmed pita pockets.

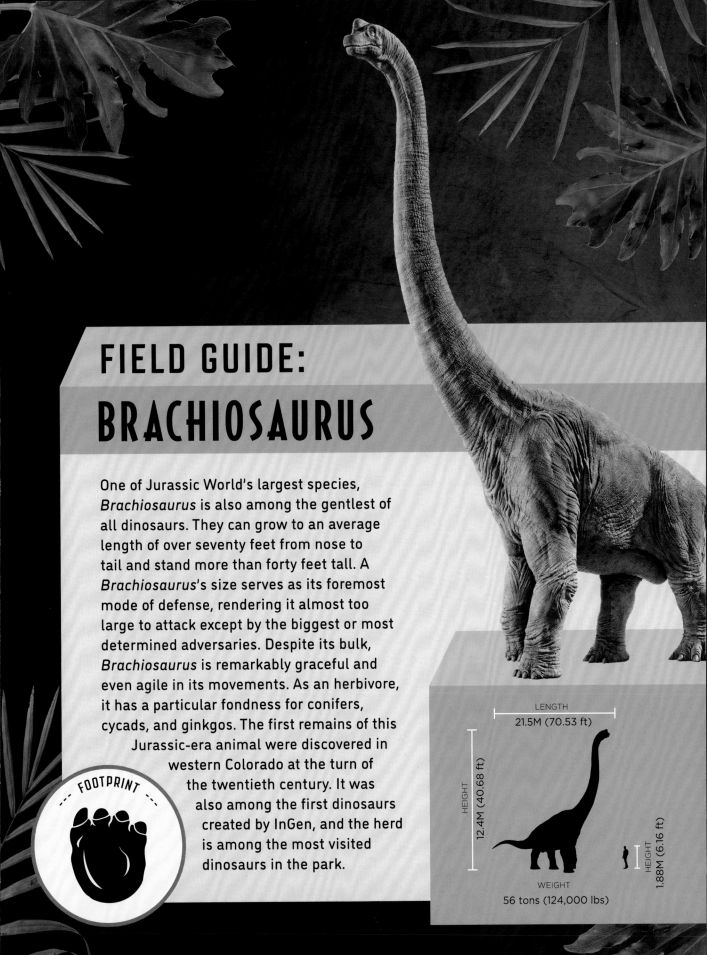

FIELD GUIDE:

BRACHIOSAURUS

One of Jurassic World's largest species, *Brachiosaurus* is also among the gentlest of all dinosaurs. They can grow to an average length of over seventy feet from nose to tail and stand more than forty feet tall. A *Brachiosaurus*'s size serves as its foremost mode of defense, rendering it almost too large to attack except by the biggest or most determined adversaries. Despite its bulk, *Brachiosaurus* is remarkably graceful and even agile in its movements. As an herbivore, it has a particular fondness for conifers, cycads, and ginkgos. The first remains of this Jurassic-era animal were discovered in western Colorado at the turn of the twentieth century. It was also among the first dinosaurs created by InGen, and the herd is among the most visited dinosaurs in the park.

--- FOOTPRINT ---

LENGTH
21.5M (70.53 ft)

HEIGHT
12.4M (40.68 ft)

HEIGHT
1.88M (6.16 ft)

WEIGHT
56 tons (124,000 lbs)

GRUBS AND GREENS

While most herbivore dinosaurs ate only plants, scientists hypothesize that some may have eaten insects as well. This interesting idea is still being investigated at Jurassic World, and along the way it inspired this tantalizing vegan dish. Our version uses beans instead of insects, blended with rainbow chard and topped with crispy fried shallots.

YIELD: 4 TO 6 SERVINGS

FOR THE FRIED SHALLOTS:
4 large shallots, sliced thin

¼ cup flour

½ teaspoon salt, plus more for sprinkling

About 1 cup oil for frying, such as corn or safflower

FOR THE GRUBS AND GREENS:
1 large bunch rainbow chard, washed and dried

1 to 2 tablespoons oil to coat the pan

4 cloves garlic, minced

½ teaspoon salt

1 cup vegetable broth

One 15-ounce can white kidney beans

SPECIAL SUPPLIES:
Fry thermometer

TIP:
Can't find white kidney beans? No problem. Substitute in any other large white bean, such as Great Northern.

TO MAKE THE FRIED SHALLOTS:

1. Add shallots to a plastic container and sprinkle with flour and salt. Seal the container with a tight-fitting lid, and shake to coat the shallots in the flour and salt. A zippable plastic bag can be used in place of the bowl and lid. Separate the shallots into ribbons.

2. Line a large plate with paper towel. In a medium-size high-sided skillet fitted with a fry thermometer, heat ¼ inch of oil to 350°F. Fry the shallots in batches for 2 to 3 minutes or until golden brown. Use tongs to pull them out of the pan, and shake off excess oil. Transfer to a paper towel-lined plate, and sprinkle with salt to taste. When all shallots have been fried, set aside.

TO MAKE THE GRUBS AND GREENS:

3. Cut the stems of the chard into ¼-inch slices, just up to where the leaves start. Set stem pieces aside. Roll the leaves loosely, and slice into thin strips.

4. In a large sauté pan on medium heat, add the oil and garlic, and sauté until garlic is fragrant, 2 to 3 minutes. Add the stems and salt, and sauté until stems are just tender, about 3 minutes. Add in the broth and the beans, and bring to a simmer. Simmer until liquid is reduced by about a third.

5. Add the chard greens to the pan on top of the bean mixture. Cover, and let steam for 3 minutes, until just wilted.

DON'T MISS

Gyrosphere Tours

GYROSPHERES
EXPERIENCE THE DINOS UPCLOSE

The wonders of Jurassic World, from the monorail to the guided tours, are amazing experiences on their own, but venturing among the dinosaurs in their natural habitat is an unrivaled adventure that can't be missed. Gyrosphere Valley spans nearly twenty square miles in which thirty species, including *Gallimimus*, are free to roam without fear of predators. As these animals are peaceful by nature, guests also have the opportunity to see them up close thanks to Jurassic World's patented Gyrosphere technology. These orb-like, two-person vehicles allow visitors to travel through the valley while observing the majestic animals. Each transparent Gyrosphere's onboard, networked computer system ensures the safety of both guests and dinosaurs. Don't worry if one of the residents gives chase, as Gyrospheres can outpace everything in the valley. Climb aboard and take a spin!

"ARMORED" ARTICHOKE PLATES

One of the most popular and recognizable dinosaurs, *Stegosaurus* is famous for the massive row of armored plates along its back as well as its deadly spiked tail. Here we pay homage to this beloved dinosaur with an artichoke dish inspired by *Stegosaurus*'s famous profile. Serve with our zesty homemade mayonnaise for an appealing appetizer that's surprisingly easy to pull off.

YIELD: 6 TO 8 SERVINGS

FOR THE PLATES:
2 large globe artichokes
½ lemon, quartered
2 cloves garlic, smashed
Several sprigs of fresh thyme
Coarse ground black pepper, to taste

FOR THE GARLIC MUSTARD AIOLI:
3 cloves garlic, minced
1 egg
Pinch of sea salt
1 cup olive oil
1 tablespoon lemon juice
2 teaspoons Dijon mustard
Fresh ground black pepper, to taste

SPECIAL SUPPLIES:
Large pot with a steamer insert

TO MAKE THE ARTICHOKE PLATES:

1. Prepare the artichokes by trimming the stems and the top inch of the leaves. Rub a lemon wedge over the cut areas to prevent discoloring.
2. Place the remaining lemon, garlic, thyme, and black pepper in a large stockpot, and fill with 2 inches of water. Put the steamer insert inside, and bring the water to a boil. Add the artichokes to the steamer, cut-side down, and reduce the heat until the water stays at a brisk simmer. Steam the artichokes for 20 to 30 minutes, or until the bottoms are fork-tender.
3. While the artichokes are cooking, prepare an ice bath by filling a bowl with cold water and ice. When the artichokes are done, use tongs to remove them from the heat and plunge them into the ice water to stop cooking. Remove immediately, and drain in a colander. Cut each artichoke into quarters. Use a teaspoon to carefully remove the choke (the fuzzy center above the heart) from each piece.

TO PREPARE THE AIOLI:

4. Add the garlic, egg, and salt to the bowl of a food processor. Blend until the egg is smooth and pale yellow, between 1 and 2 minutes. Add the olive oil in a slow, thin, steady stream.
5. Once the oil is incorporated, transfer to a small bowl, and add the lemon juice, mustard, and black pepper. Stir gently to combine.
6. Serve the quartered artichokes with a small dish of the aioli for dipping, and a discard bowl for leaves.

DATE DROPS

Dates have been around for a long time—about fifty million years, in fact, according to some fossil records. Maybe they're not as old as dinosaurs, but they're still old enough to be considered prehistoric. Here, they're at the heart of this tasty cookie creation, which can easily be made gluten-free with the right kind of oats.

YIELD: ABOUT 18 DROPS

2 cups whole pecans, divided

1 cup old-fashioned oats, gluten-free if preferred

1 cup pitted dates

3 very ripe bananas

½ teaspoon kosher salt

1 teaspoon vanilla bean paste

½ teaspoon cinnamon

SPECIAL SUPPLIES:

1½-inch cookie scoop

1. Preheat the oven to 375°F. Prepare two cookie sheets by lining them with a silicone baking mat or parchment paper. Sort through the pecans, and pull out 18 nice-looking ones. Reserve these for the tops of your date drops.
2. Heat a dry, medium-size skillet on medium-high until very hot. Turn off the heat, and add the remaining nuts to the pan. Toast the nuts, stirring gently until fragrant, about 3 minutes.
3. Add oats to a food processor, and pulse 2 or 3 times to create the base for your dough. Add dates and toasted pecans, and pulse a few more times, until the individual pieces are about the size of a pea. Add the bananas, and run the processor until the dough comes together, 1 minute or less.
4. Turn off the processor, and scrape down the sides of the bowl. Add the salt, vanilla paste, and cinnamon, and run until just combined.
5. Using the cookie scoop, scoop mounds of the dough onto the prepared cookie sheets about 1 inch apart. Press a whole pecan into the top of each one. Bake for 15 to 20 minutes, or until the edges start to brown. Remove to a wire rack to cool—the drops will be soft but firm up as they cool. Serve immediately or store in an airtight container for 2 to 3 days.

FIELD GUIDE:
TRICERATOPS

Named for the pair of large horns above their eyes accompanied by a smaller horn jutting from the nose, *Triceratops* ("Three-Horned Face") roamed the American Midwest as well as parts of southern Canada sixty-six million years ago. It was among the last of the dinosaurs, surviving until the late Cretaceous Period. Remains of the first known specimen were found in 1877 near Denver, Colorado, and discoverers initially believed it was a bison. Subsequent finds disproved this theory and instead served to identify a whole new family of dinosaurs: *Ceratops*. Although *Triceratops* is an herbivore, and therefore will not attack another dinosaur with the intent of eating it, it has been known to demonstrate aggressive behavior in other situations, and fights between two or more *Triceratops* are not uncommon. On the other hand, baby *Triceratops* are surprisingly docile and are a popular attraction for younger visitors to the park's Gentle Giants Petting Zoo. *Triceratops* is a very indiscriminate eater who will consume any and all plants within reach, including berries and other vegetation that might make it ill. Jurassic World trainers and other support staff have to stay on their toes to ensure that these voracious plant eaters stay healthy and strong!

FOOTPRINT

LENGTH
8.9M (29.19 ft)

HEIGHT
3.6M (11.81 ft)

HEIGHT
1.88M (6.16 ft)

WEIGHT
12 tons (22,000 lbs)

FOSSILIZED FLORA PASTRY PUFFS

Before Jurassic World made it possible to study the flora and fauna of prehistoric times in the "here and now," paleobotanists used the fossils of ancient plant specimens to draw conclusions about what the planet had been like as far back as 165 million years ago. Inspired by the swirly fossils of split pine cones, these delicious puff pastry spirals feature goat cheese and pine nuts accented with olive oil, lemon, and other seasonings, which really draw out the sharp, savory flavor.

YIELD: ABOUT 45 TO 60 SPIRALS

1 package frozen puff pastry
8 ounces fresh goat cheese
Zest and juice of 1 lemon
1 tablespoon fresh thyme leaves
1 tablespoon olive oil
¼ teaspoon sea salt
Fresh ground black pepper, to taste
1 cup pine nuts, about 5 ounces, toasted

1. Defrost the puff pastry according to package directions. Prepare a cookie sheet by lining it with parchment paper.
2. While the puff pastry is thawing, prepare the filling. Combine all the ingredients except the pine nuts, and whip until a spreadable, light consistency has been reached, about 1 to 2 minutes.
3. Roll out each sheet of puff pastry to roughly 11 by 12 inches. Spread half the goat cheese mixture over each piece, and sprinkle with half the pine nuts, pressing the nuts into the cheese. Starting at the long edge, roll each piece tightly into a log. Place both logs on the prepared cookie sheet and transfer to the freezer. Freeze for 30 minutes.
4. Preheat the oven to 400°F. Prepare two cookie sheets by lining with silicone baking mats or parchment paper.
5. Remove one log from the freezer, and cut into ¼-inch slices. Place slices on the prepared baking sheets, and bake for 15 to 20 minutes, or until golden and crispy. Repeat with the second log.
6. Cool the slices on a wire rack for 3 to 5 minutes, and serve warm.

TIP:

Unbaked slices can be frozen on a cookie sheet and then stored in the freezer in an airtight container until needed. Baked spirals can be stored in an airtight container at room temperature for 2 to 3 days and re-crisped in a 350°F oven for 3 to 5 minutes.

FRUIT 'N' LEAVES SALAD

Looking for a light, sweet side dish for a summer meal? Take a leaf out of *Gallimimus*'s book. A hefty part of the *Gallimimus* diet includes fresh fruit and leafy greens, inspiring this refreshing salad of seasonal fruits partnered with microgreens and topped with a tangy citrus dressing.

YIELD: 6 TO 8 SERVINGS

FOR THE DRESSING:
Juice of 1 lime
Juice of ½ lemon
2 tablespoons honey
1 large sprig of fresh mint

FOR THE FRUIT SALAD:
2 apples
2 plums
2 peaches
2 kiwis
1 mango
1 bunch of microgreens, such as pea, beet, or radish

TO MAKE THE DRESSING:

1. Combine all the ingredients, except the mint sprig in a small saucepan, and bring to a boil over medium-high heat. Remove the pan from the heat immediately, add the mint sprig, and allow to cool completely.

TO MAKE THE SALAD:

2. Place the cooled dressing in the bottom of a large bowl. Cut the fruit into bite-size pieces in the order they appear in the ingredients list, and add them to the bowl. As you add each new bunch of fruit, give the salad a quick toss to incorporate the new fruit and coat it in the dressing.
3. When all the fruit has been incorporated, cover the salad with plastic wrap and chill in the refrigerator until ready to serve.
4. Garnish salad with the microgreens, and serve.

FIELD GUIDE:
GALLIMIMUS

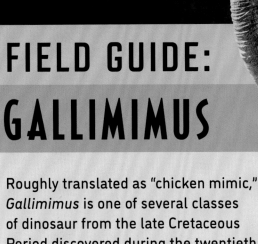

Roughly translated as "chicken mimic," *Gallimimus* is one of several classes of dinosaur from the late Cretaceous Period discovered during the twentieth century. The first remains were among numerous specimens found in the early 1960s in the Gobi Desert region of Mongolia. Standing at an average of nine feet tall, *Gallimimus* is about fifteen feet long, and nearly half of that length belongs to its tail. While it prefers a diet of fruits and leaves, *Gallimimus* is an omnivore and will also eat whatever small mammals or reptiles it finds. Its primary mode of defense is a tendency to move in herds as well as its ability to run at speeds exceeding twenty miles per hour. Park guests can see this for themselves while touring the Gyrosphere Valley. While our specimens are generally shy, interactions with trainers as well as guests at our Gentle Giants Petting Zoo have revealed an occasional impulse toward playful behavior.

--- FOOTPRINT ---

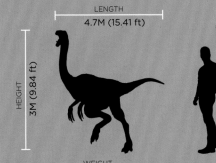

LENGTH
4.7M (15.41 ft)

HEIGHT
3M (9.84 ft)

HEIGHT
1.88M (6.16 ft)

WEIGHT
450 kg (1,000 lbs)

SPINY FIG SKEWERS

Figs have existed in one form or another since at least the Cretaceous Period—perhaps as far back as sixty-five million years ago. Their honey-like sweetness pairs perfectly with aromatic rosemary, making these roasted fig skewers as scrumptious as they are visually striking. One of the slightly fancier vegetarian dishes at Jurassic World, this dish is guaranteed to be as much of a hit at your next dinner party as they are here in the park.

YIELD: 6 TO 8 SERVINGS

¼ cup honey

1 tablespoon balsamic vinegar

Six 6- to 8-inch-long rosemary stalks

1 basket of figs, or about 12 ounces, stems trimmed

¼ cup roasted, unsalted, shelled pistachios, coarsely chopped

¾ cup crème fraîche or plain Greek yogurt, for serving

SPECIAL SUPPLIES:

Kitchen shears

1. Preheat the oven to 375°F, and line a rimmed baking sheet with parchment paper.
2. Whisk the honey and balsamic vinegar together, and set aside.
3. Pull the leaves from the bottom of each rosemary stalk, exposing about 3 inches. Trim the ends with kitchen shears. Thread 3 to 4 figs onto each rosemary skewer (it's okay if they slide over the leaves a bit, but they should stay mainly on the stem). Place the skewers on the baking sheet, and roast for 5 minutes. Remove the skewers from the oven, and brush the figs with the honey mixture. Return the sheet to the oven, and roast another 5 minutes.
4. Mix the pistachios into the remaining honey mixture. Drizzle the honeyed pistachios over the figs, and roast another 3 minutes. Remove from the oven, and allow to cool on the sheet for 3 to 5 minutes.
5. Serve over crème fraîche or plain Greek yogurt.

SECRET MENU

Remove the figs from the spines and use them to top the Chorreadas de Nublar (page 76) for a sweet breakfast treat.

TIP:

Long rosemary is usually found in a tied bunch in grocery stores rather than in a blister pack. If you can't find longer rosemary stalks, thread the figs onto wooden skewers and lay them on top of rosemary sprigs to infuse with flavor.

Beef-, pork-, and poultry-based dishes from the heart of T. Rex Kingdom

Some of the most unforgettable dinosaurs you'll meet at Jurassic World are the carnivores: *Carnotaurus*, *Velociraptor*, and—of course—*Tyrannosaurus rex*. These fierce predators are as awe-inspiring as they are dangerous, and our staff goes to great lengths to ensure their safety as well as that of everyone visiting the island. Each of these magnificents animals requires a substantial diet of meat. In honor of their voracious appetites, in this section we share some of the park's most hearty recipes for human meat-eaters, including brined turkey legs, pork belly sliders, and a Mediterranean-inspired hamburger with homemade pickled red onions.

THE ULTIMATE CARNIVORE'S BURGER

Jurassic World is home to some of the most magnificent carnivores on Earth... and one of the most magnificent burgers. Named for our majestic meat eaters, our Mediterranean-inspired Ultimate Carnivore's Burger, served daily throughout T. Rex Kingdom, features not one meat, but three, so guests can enjoy the maximum carnivore experience.

YIELD: 6 BURGERS

FOR THE PATTIES:
1 pound ground beef
1 pound ground lamb
1 teaspoon sea salt
½ teaspoon fresh ground black pepper
1 tablespoon of Dijon mustard
6 thin slices of pancetta (about 2 ounces)

FOR THE FETA TOPPING:
6 ounces crumbled feta
1 tablespoon minced fresh mint leaves
2 tablespoons olive oil
Fresh ground black pepper, to taste

CONTINUED ON PAGE 40

FOR THE PICKLED RED ONIONS:

1 red onion, thinly sliced

1 cup white vinegar

½ cup water

¼ cup balsamic vinegar

1 tablespoon molasses

¼ cup packed light brown sugar

1½ tablespoons whole peppercorns

1½ tablespoons coriander seeds

1 tablespoon kosher salt

Pinch of red pepper flakes

SPECIAL SUPPLIES:

16-ounce canning jar with lid, sterilized

TO SERVE:

6 burger buns, toasted

½ cup mayonnaise or Garlic Mustard Aioli (page 27)

TO MAKE THE PICKLED ONIONS:

1. Press the onions down in the canning jar, and set aside.
2. In a small saucepan, bring the rest of the ingredients to a boil over medium-high heat. Once boiling, remove the pan from the heat, and pour the mixture into the jar over the onions, making sure all the onions are submerged. Put the lid on the jar and allow to cool to room temperature.
3. Transfer to the refrigerator, and chill for least 1 hour or overnight. The onions will last in the refrigerator for up to 2 weeks.

TO MAKE THE FETA TOPPING:

4. In a medium bowl, gently toss the feta crumbles with the mint leaves, olive oil, and black pepper to taste. Set aside.

TO MAKE THE BURGERS:

5. In a large bowl, combine the beef and lamb, salt, pepper, and mustard, and mix by hand until completely combined. Grill the patties until desired doneness, 140°F for medium, 155°F for medium well.
6. While burgers are grilling, render the slices of pancetta by cooking over medium heat for 8 to 10 minutes. Turn to crisp on both sides, and set aside on a plate lined with paper towels.

TO ASSEMBLE THE BURGERS:

7. Spread the mayonnaise or garlic aioli on both sides of each bun, about 1 tablespoon per bun. Put a crisped piece of pancetta on the bottom bun and top with a burger patty.
8. Place about a ¼ cup of the feta cheese mixture on top of each patty, and top that with pickled onion. Serve with Compy Pack Curly Fries (page 117) or Fossilized Potato Spirals (page 130).

FIELD GUIDE:
TYRANNOSAURUS REX

Jurassic World's most famous resident, *Tyrannosaurus rex*, is among the strongest and fiercest carnivores. While it is not the largest of the dinosaurs, the "King Tyrant Lizard" is believed to have possessed strong intelligence—a theory strengthened by observation of the park's resident specimen. The *T. rex* roamed (and ruled!) over what is now the southwestern and midwestern United States and central Canada at the end of the Cretaceous Period, and its first remains were discovered in the 1870s near Golden, Colorado. An apex predator, it can grow to over forty feet in length and stand nearly twenty feet tall. It's as fast as it is vicious. In fact, Jurassic World staff has clocked our *T. rex* running at speeds in excess of thirty miles per hour. In the Cretaceous Period, *T. rex*'s diet was basically other dinosaurs, along with whatever other meat it could find. In Jurassic World, our *T. rex*'s diet consists of smaller mammals like goats. Visitors can observe *T. rex*'s rather "spirited" eating habits every two hours in T. Rex Kingdom.

FOOTPRINT

LENGTH
13.5M (44.29 ft)

HEIGHT
5.2M (17.06 ft)

HEIGHT
1.88M (6.16 ft)

WEIGHT
8.4 tonnes (18,518 lbs)

SKEWERED PINEAPPLE PORK TACOS

Satisfy the biggest of appetites with a massive spit of roasted pork fit for a *Tyrannosaurus rex*. The perfect showstopping centerpiece for a party of meat eaters, the pork is cooked with tangy pineapple and sliced fresh and hot off the skewer. Serve the tacos with fresh corn tortillas and all the fixings!

YIELD: 8 SERVINGS

1 cup pineapple juice

1 cup white wine vinegar

1 tablespoon kosher salt

2 teaspoons fresh ground black pepper

1 tablespoon garlic powder

1 tablespoon dried oregano

1 teaspoon ground coriander

1 teaspoon ground cumin

2 teaspoons chili powder

1 teaspoon paprika

3 tablespoons canned chipotle peppers in adobo sauce, finely chopped

5 pounds boneless pork shoulder, cut into ½-inch slices

1 fresh pineapple

Tortillas, for serving

Cotija cheese, for serving

Chopped white onion, for serving

Sliced avocado, for serving

SPECIAL SUPPLIES:

Thick wooden or metal skewer

Roasting pan, with a rack that will fit inside it

1. In a container large enough to hold all the pork, whisk together the pineapple juice, white wine vinegar, kosher salt, black pepper, garlic powder, oregano, coriander, cumin, chili powder, paprika, and chipotle peppers until combined. Add the pork to the container, turning the pieces to coat. Cover and transfer to the refrigerator to marinate for at least 4 hours or overnight, turning pork pieces at least once during that time.

2. Preheat the oven to 350°F. Place the oven rack in the center of the oven. Cover a rimmed baking pan in foil, and place a rack inside it.

3. Remove the stem of the pineapple. Slice a 1-inch piece off the bottom and top of the pineapple, and set them aside. Peel and core the rest of the pineapple, and cut the fruit into large pieces. Push the dull end of the skewer into the fleshy side of the bottom piece of the pineapple.

4. Thread each slice of pork onto the skewer, continuing until all the pork is threaded. Finish off the skewer with the top piece of pineapple, creating two "wheels" on the ends. Place the pork spit onto the rack in the roasting pan, placing the pineapple wheels into the spaces of the rack to keep the pork elevated. Toss the remaining pineapple pieces in the marinade, and arrange around the pork. Brush additional marinade over the pork, and then discard any extra marinade.

5. Roast the pork for 1½ hours, or until the outside has a good char and the internal temperature is 150°F. During that time, turn the pork spit and baste with the pan juices every half hour.

6. Remove from the oven and let rest 10 to 15 minutes. To carve, use a chef's knife to slice the meat off the sides of the tower and then slide the leftover meat off the skewer. Arrange the meat and roasted pineapple on a serving platter. Serve with warm tortillas, Cotija cheese, chopped onion, and sliced avocado as desired.

GOOD HUNTING PORK BELLY SLIDERS

Served with a tangy, spicy sauce, these succulent pork belly sliders are good hunting! Just remember to keep an eye out for scavengers or you might find your "prey" has disappeared . . .

YIELD: 6 SERVINGS OR 12 SLIDERS

FOR THE SAUCE:

2 tablespoons tamarind paste

1 teaspoon chili adobo sauce, from a can of chipotle peppers with adobo sauce

3 tablespoons packed dark brown sugar

½ cup orange juice

½ teaspoon garlic powder

½ teaspoon salt

Fresh ground black pepper, to taste

FOR THE SLIDERS:

1-pound piece of pork belly, cross-hatched

2 teaspoons salt

1 tablespoon vegetable oil

12 slider buns, toasted

12 small pieces of butter lettuce, from the center of a head of butter lettuce

12 thin slices of red onion, about ½ an onion

¼ cup cilantro leaves, optional

TO MAKE THE SAUCE:

1. Combine all the ingredients in a small saucepan, and bring to a simmer over medium heat. Simmer 5 to 8 minutes, until the sauce is thick enough to coat the back of a spoon. Remove from the heat, and set aside to cool.

TO MAKE THE PORK:

2. Rub the pork with 2 teaspoons salt, using 1 teaspoon for each side. Let sit for 10 minutes. Slice into ½-inch-thick slices, and toss in a large bowl with 2 tablespoons of the sauce and vegetable oil. Transfer to the refrigerator, and let marinate for at least 30 minutes or up to a few hours. Reserve the remaining sauce (at least 3 tablespoons) for spreading on the buns.

3. In a nonstick skillet over medium-high heat, cook the pork belly in small batches (be careful not to overcrowd the pan) for 3 to 4 minutes on each side, until both sides are well charred. Brush with the remaining marinade while cooking. Discard the fat drippings between batches.

TO ASSEMBLE:

4. Brush the bottom bun with sauce, top with a lettuce leaf, 2 pieces of pork, onion, and cilantro leaves (if using). Finish the slider with the top bun, and serve.

SECRET MENU

Top your sliders with the pickled onions from the Ultimate Carnivore's Burger (page 39) instead of the red onion to add a bit of tang.

RAPTOR-WORTHY WRAPS

Velociraptors may be small for a carnivorous dinosaur, but they are not to be underestimated—just like this lip-smacking wrap, which features chicken marinated in spicy homemade ketchup. A popular sandwich alternative, this wrap features an exquisite blend of ingredients and flavors that make it an ideal meal for lunch or dinner.

YIELD: 8 WRAPS

FOR THE CHICKEN:

2 pounds boneless, skinless chicken thighs

½ cup Spicy Ketchup (page 49)

FOR THE SLAW:

½ red onion, thinly sliced

1½ cups shredded red cabbage, about half a head

1 cucumber, peeled and cut into matchsticks

1 tablespoon rice wine vinegar

1 teaspoon sea salt

FOR THE SAUCE:

1 cup sour cream

1 tablespoon minced fresh mint leaves

Juice of ½ lemon

½ teaspoon sea salt

½ teaspoon garlic powder

Fresh ground black pepper, to taste

8 large spinach or flour tortillas

2 Roma tomatoes, sliced

1 avocado, sliced

1. In a large bowl or plastic bag, toss the chicken in the Spicy Ketchup and transfer to the refrigerator to marinate, for 25 minutes to 1 hour.
2. While the chicken is marinating, prepare the slaw by tossing all the ingredients together in a large bowl. In a separate medium bowl, prepare the sauce by thoroughly mixing all the ingredients together. Transfer both slaw and sauce to the refrigerator until ready to serve.
3. Preheat the grill to 375°F.
4. Grill the chicken for 10 to 15 minutes, or until the internal temp is 165°F. Remove and let rest on a plate for 5 to 10 minutes, before cutting into strips. While the chicken is resting, briefly cook each tortilla in a large, dry skillet over medium heat, slightly toasting each side.

TO ASSEMBLE:

5. Place about ½ cup of slaw along the bottom third of a tortilla, and top with several strips of chicken. Add tomato and avocado slices, plus a generous drizzle of sauce. Fold up the bottom, then both sides in firmly against the filling, then roll to close the wrap. Repeat with the remaining tortillas.
6. Slice each wrap down the middle on an angle and serve with more sauce, if desired.

SECRET MENU:

Love wraps, but not a carnivore? Substitute a few Jurassic Fritters for the chicken in this dish to create a delicious herbivore-friendly meal.

FIELD GUIDE:
VELOCIRAPTOR

It might not be anywhere near the biggest of the dinosaurs, but the *Velociraptor* is a formidable breed. Typically growing to an average height of around six feet, *Velociraptors* compensate for their small size with wickedly sharp claws, rows of razor-like teeth, and tremendous speed. Since the initial discovery of raptor fossils in 1923 in Mongolia, theories about this animal's habits and capabilities have abounded. InGen's success at engineering *Velociraptors* has laid many of these ideas to rest while, at the same time, revealing many fascinating truths. Through our program, we've learned that raptors are not only highly intelligent but also very adaptable. They're capable of rapid learning and acclimating to new situations. This makes them formidable hunters in the wild, subsisting on all manner of smaller dinosaurs. When working in packs, *Velociraptors* can and do challenge larger animals—and they often win.

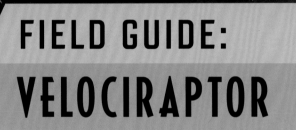

--- FOOTPRINT ---

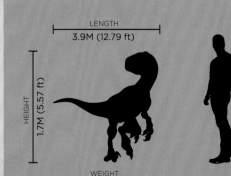

LENGTH
3.9M (12.79 ft)

HEIGHT
1.7M (5.57 ft)

HEIGHT
1.88M (6.16 ft)

WEIGHT
226 kg (500 lbs)

SERVED
WITH COMPY PACK
CURLY FRIES
(PAGE 117)

THE JURASSIC DOG

At Jurassic World, we take a classic hot dog and give it a daring subtropical twist with some spicy ketchup and quick-pickled veggies inspired by local Costa Rican flavors.

YIELD: 8 LOADED DOGS

FOR THE SPICY KETCHUP:

Sauce from one 7-ounce can chipotle peppers in adobo sauce (reserve peppers for future use if desired)

One 6-ounce can tomato paste

One 15-ounce can tomato sauce

¼ cup packed dark brown sugar

¼ cup honey

1 tablespoon Worcestershire sauce

FOR THE QUICK PICKLES:

4 sprigs of cilantro, divided

4 small cloves garlic, peeled, divided

2 tablespoons whole mixed peppercorns, divided

1 red onion, thinly sliced

1 jalapeño, sliced in thin rounds

2 carrots, sliced on an angle, ½-inch thick

4 radishes, quartered, or cut into eighths if large

¼ head cauliflower, broken into small florets

1 cup water

¾ cup white vinegar

2 teaspoons salt

2 tablespoons Serrano Orange Syrup (p 134)

FOR THE DOGS:

8 all-beef hot dogs, or dogs of choice

8 large hot dog buns

SPECIAL SUPPLIES:

2 large mason jars with tight-fitting lids, clean and dry

TO MAKE THE SPICY KETCHUP:

1. Remove the peppers from the can of adobo sauce and store in the refrigerator for future recipes, if desired. Combine the adobo sauce with the rest of the ingredients in a small saucepan over medium heat. Bring to a simmer, turn the heat down to medium-low, and simmer sauce for 20 to 30 minutes until smooth and slightly thickened.

2. Allow to cool completely before storing in an airtight container in the refrigerator for up to 2 weeks. Makes about 3 cups.

TO MAKE THE QUICK PICKLES:

3. Place 2 sprigs of cilantro, 2 garlic cloves, and 1 tablespoon of peppercorns into each mason jar. In a large bowl, toss together the red onion, jalapeño, carrots, radishes, and cauliflower until well mixed, then divide them between the two mason jars, packing them tightly.

4. In a small saucepan over high heat, bring the water, vinegar, salt, and syrup to a boil for 1 to 2 minutes, by which time the salt should have dissolved. Carefully pour the mixture over the vegetables, filling up each jar. Cover each jar, and allow to cool to room temperature. Transfer to the refrigerator and chill for least 1 hour or overnight. At this point, the pickles will last in the refrigerated for up to 2 weeks.

TO MAKE THE HOG DOGS:

5. Grill the hot dogs according to your preferences and toast the buns on the grill or in the oven. Once the dogs and buns are ready, spread some of the Spicy Ketchup on the bottom of each bun, place a hot dog on top, and then top with the pickled vegetables. Serve immediately.

T. REX KINGDOM TURKEY LEG

Nothing says "I'm in T. Rex Kingdom now" quite like wielding a scrumptiously prepared turkey leg as you wander the park, observing the fascinating, adrenaline-inducing meat eaters that live there. Brined and then slowly roasted with a delectable mix of spices, these turkey legs are a Jurassic World special that we're excited to share with you now.

YIELD: 8 SERVINGS

24 cups water

4 cups kosher salt

3 bay leaves

1 bulb garlic, halved crosswise, no peeling necessary

1 tablespoon black peppercorns

½ tablespoon coriander seeds

8 cups ice

4 pounds turkey drumsticks and/or thighs

6 tablespoons unsalted butter, softened

1. In a very large pot, big enough to hold 2 gallons of water and the turkey meat, combine 12 cups of the water, the salt, and the spices. Bring to a boil, and cook until all the salt is dissolved. Remove from heat, and add 12 more cups of water and the ice, and allow to cool completely.

2. When the brine is completely cool, add the turkey legs and/or thighs. If necessary, place a plate directly over the legs and thighs in the brine to weigh them down (you want to make sure they remain completely submerged throughout the brining process). Alternatively, you can transfer both the brine and turkey to a large, zippable bag. Place the pot (or bag, if using) in the refrigerator, and allow the turkey to brine for 4 hours. After 4 hours, remove the turkey from the brine, pat dry, and set aside while preheating the oven. Discard the brine.

3. Preheat the oven to 450°F.

4. Place a baking rack inside a rimmed baking sheet, arrange the turkey pieces on the rack, and rub all over with the butter. Roast for 30 minutes. Reduce the heat to 325°F, and baste the turkey with the butter and juices. Roast another 15 minutes before checking the internal temperature. Remove the turkey from the oven when it has reached 165°F. Tent with foil and allow to rest for 20 minutes. The temp will continue to rise as it rests. Serve hot, and feel free to enjoy on the go.

FIELD GUIDE:
CARNOTAURUS

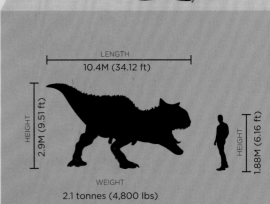

Following its discovery in 1984, the *Carnotaurus* fossil excavated from the Chubut Province in Argentina was the only known representative of its species until InGen's team of genetic engineers went to work. Though similar in general physiology to *Tyrannosaurus rex*, the *Carnotaurus* is defined by a much smaller head and shorter arms. While it can reach well over thirty feet in length, its modest nine-foot height prevents it from taking on larger and more formidable opponents. However, its muscular hind legs allow it to achieve running speeds rivaling *T. rex*'s. They also offer *Carnotaurus* the ability to launch powerful kicks against adversaries, giving it at least some advantage in a fight. Despite this, it prefers to size up potential prey before moving in for the strike, often chasing down smaller dinosaurs in addition to other animals that serve its carnivorous dietary needs. It then consumes its meal with haste before running off to avoid challenges from larger predators.

--- FOOTPRINT ---

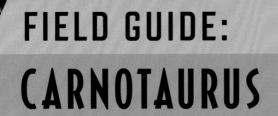

LENGTH
10.4M (34.12 ft)

HEIGHT
2.9M (9.51 ft)

HEIGHT
1.88M (6.16 ft)

WEIGHT
2.1 tonnes (4,800 lbs)

EGG THIEF OMELET

Oviraptor, meaning "egg thief," originally got its name because scientists assumed it was stealing and eating eggs. They later learned that the fossils they'd found were actually nesting atop their *own* eggs, not stealing others. Nevertheless, the name stuck. This formidable omelet named in its honor uses a grand total of one dozen eggs, making for an easy, hearty brunch big enough to feed every raptor in your social group.

YIELD: 1 OMELET FOR A CROWD! (8 SERVINGS)

2 tablespoons unsalted butter, melted

1 cup finely shredded Monterey jack cheese (about 5 ounces)

1 cup grated Parmesan cheese (about 5 ounces)

1 teaspoon fresh ground black pepper

2 tablespoons snipped chives

12 eggs

1 cup heavy cream

1 cup milk

6 ounces sliced prosciutto

SPECIAL SUPPLIES:
One 1-by-17-inch rimmed baking sheet

1. Preheat the oven to 350°F. Line the baking sheet with parchment paper, leaving a 2-inch overhang on both ends, and brush with melted butter.
2. Mix the cheeses, black pepper, and chives in a small bowl, and set aside.
3. In a large bowl, whisk together the eggs, cream, and milk until homogeneous. Add most of the cheese mixture, reserving ½ cup, to the egg mixture and mix until just combined. Place the prepared baking sheet onto the center rack of the oven, and carefully pour the egg mixture onto it. Bake for 15 to 20 minutes, or until the egg is puffed and firm.
4. While the omelet is baking, heat a medium dry skillet on medium heat. In single-layer batches, crisp each piece of prosciutto on both sides, about 1 to 2 minutes a side. Transfer to a plate lined with paper towel to drain and rest. When the omelet is set, remove it from the oven, sprinkle with the remaining cheese mixture, and cover with a single layer of crisped prosciutto.
5. Cover the baking sheet in foil, and let rest for 3 to 5 minutes. Remove foil, and use the overhanging parchment to lift the omelet to a cutting board. Starting at one of the short ends, lift the parchment and use it to help tightly roll up the omelet, pulling the parchment back as you go so it does not get caught in the roll. Cut into slices, and serve warm.

TIP:
Leftover slices can be stored in the refrigerator and served cold the next day or warmed gently in a 300°F oven.

FIELD NOTES:
Oviraptor is an omnivore who feeds on plants, eggs, and even small vertebrates, despite the fact that it has almost no teeth.

YAKITORI SPINES

A popular snack or appetizer in Japan, these skewered chicken strips are often prepared using a variety of sauces and seasonings. For our park's version, *Spinosaurus*, with its distinctive array of neural spines jutting up along its backbone, inspires our presentation, providing an enticing display and a uniquely themed spin on this quick-to-prepare yet satisfying street food.

YIELD: 4 SERVINGS AS AN ENTRÉE, OR 6 TO 8 AS AN APPETIZER

½ cup soy sauce

½ cup mirin

1 tablespoon sesame oil

3 tablespoons packed light brown sugar

3 cloves garlic, roughly chopped

Two 2-inch pieces of ginger, peeled and thickly sliced

3 scallions, cut into 1-inch pieces, using both the white and light green parts

2 pounds boneless, skinless chicken thighs, cut into long strips about 2 inches wide

½ teaspoon fresh ground black pepper

1 egg

4 ounces panko bread crumbs, about ½ a box

SPECIAL SUPPLIES:

About 12 wooden skewers, soaked in water for 30 minutes

1. In a small saucepan over medium heat, bring soy sauce, mirin, sesame oil, and brown sugar to a boil, stirring until sugar dissolves, about 1 minute. Remove from heat, and stir in garlic, ginger, and scallions. Set aside to cool.

2. Add the chicken to a container with a tight-fitting lid, or a large zippable plastic bag, and season with black pepper. Pour half the sauce mixture over the chicken, cover, and refrigerate for 4 to 6 hours. Refrigerate the remaining sauce as well.

3. Preheat the oven to 375°F. Prepare two baking sheets by lining them with parchment paper.

4. Remove the chicken from the marinade, and set it aside on a plate. Use a slotted spoon to remove the aromatics from the marinade, and discard them.

5. To set up the breading station, whisk the egg into the marinade and pour the panko bread crumbs into a separate shallow dish. Dip each piece of chicken into the egg wash and thread it onto a skewer (you should have about 3 pieces per skewer). Dredge the skewers in panko on both sides and place on the baking sheet.

6. Bake the skewers for 15 minutes, then turn them over and bake 5 to 10 more, until cooked through and golden. Chicken should reach an internal temperature of 165 when done. Remove from the oven and set aside.

7. While chicken is baking, remove the remaining sauce from the refrigerator and use a slotted spoon to remove and discard the aromatics. Heat the sauce in a small saucepan over medium heat until warm, around 5 minutes. Serve on the side to drizzle or dip.

Tyrannosaurus Rex Kingdom

Dinosaur royalty needs a realm to rule, so naturally *Tyrannosaurus rex* gets its very own kingdom within Jurassic World. One of the park's first residents is also one of its most popular attractions, drawing thousands of guests each day to observe this most feared of the dinosaurs in the closest possible re-creation of its original environment. Viewing ports along an enclosed walkway constructed to resemble the trunk of a massive fallen tree provide a near-eye-level view of *T. rex* as it roams its paddock. It's also the perfect vantage point to take in one of the feedings that occur every two hours. Visitors should know that *T. rex* feeds on live animals like cows and goats, and observing its eating habits can be disturbing for first-time viewers. Those looking to enhance the experience even further can purchase tickets to help with one of the feedings conducted during the park's normal operating hours. Guests who opt for this once-in-a-lifetime experience—after attending a mandatory safety briefing and signing a waiver—work alongside our trained technicians in choosing meat and placing it in *T. rex*'s paddock.

TYRANNOSAURUS REX KINGDOM

Fish and other seafood inspired by the Jurassic World Lagoon

The Costa Rican region of the Pacific Ocean provides Isla Nublar with a wealth of opportunities for sea-based cuisine inspired by Jurassic World's piscivore, or "fish-eating," dinosaurs. While this of course includes *Mosasaurus* and other denizens of the Jurassic World Lagoon, even land-based residents like *Baryonyx* and avians such as *Pteranodon* dine on salty sea delights. The diversity of aquatic delicacies in the area influences a variety of recipes and presentations to satisfy even the most discerning diners. See the following pages for a few park favorites.

SHRIMP À LA ISLA NUBLAR

Raw or cooked, cold or hot, served as an appetizer or featured as the star ingredient in a main course, shrimp are incredibly versatile. Here we present one of our most popular shrimp dishes, which features a Central American flavor profile and is sure to please as either a starter or an entrée.

YIELD: 6 SERVINGS AS AN ENTRÉE OR 12 AS AN APPETIZER

1½ pounds large shrimp, 26 to 30 count, peeled and deveined, with tails left on

Juice of 1 lime

½ teaspoon sea salt

3 tablespoons olive oil

⅓ cup pitted dates, chopped

3 tablespoons pepper jelly

1. In a large bowl, toss the shrimp with lime juice and salt. Heat a large skillet on medium high heat. Add the olive oil, shrimp, and juices, and sauté until almost done, 2 to 3 minutes. Add the dates and pepper jelly and give the pan a quick stir to make sure everything is mixed.

2. Continue to sauté until the shrimp are completely cooked—pink and opaque—and the sauce has reduced to a sticky glaze, another 2 to 3 minutes.

3. Serve shrimp alone as an appetizer or over pasta topped with Iguanodon Avocado Pesto (page 21).

SERVED WITH IGUANODON AVOCADO PESTO
(PAGE 21)

"FEEDING TIME" FISH STICKS

Fish sticks earn a nearly universal thumbs-up from young snack seekers, and our version is a highlight of kids' menus throughout the park. When it's "feeding time" for your little dinosaur lovers, this is one dish you can be sure they'll snap right up.

YIELD: 4 TO 6 SERVINGS

FOR THE SAUCE:
2 tablespoons mayonnaise
1 tablespoon chopped capers
Juice of ½ lemon
Fresh ground black pepper, to taste

FOR THE FISH STICKS:
1 pound of tilapia or other white fish, cut into 1-by-3-inch pieces
1 teaspoon salt, plus more for sprinkling
1 cup cake flour
2 eggs, beaten
½ teaspoon dried dill
1 cup crushed cornflakes
1 teaspoon onion powder
Fresh ground black pepper, to taste

TO MAKE THE SAUCE:

1. In a small bowl, whisk together all the ingredients. Chill in the refrigerator until ready to serve.

TO MAKE THE FISH STICKS:

2. Place a cookie sheet in the oven and preheat to 400°F (you want both the oven and the sheet to be preheated).
3. Lay your fish strips out on a cutting board or cookie sheet, and sprinkle them lightly with salt. Set up the breading station with 3 shallow bowls: one with cake flour, one with the whisked egg and dill, and one with the cornflakes, onion powder, salt, and black pepper.
4. Dredge each piece of fish in the cake flour, then the egg mixture, then the cornflakes, pressing gently as needed to make the cornflakes adhere.
5. Carefully place the breaded fish sticks on the preheated cookie sheet, and bake for 6 minutes, flip, and bake another 6 to 10 minutes, or until firm. Serve warm with sauce.

FIELD GUIDE:
MOSASAURUS

While *Tyrannosaurus rex* may rule Jurassic World on land, the lagoon in the center of the park belongs to *Mosasaurus*. *Mosasaurus* represents one of the earliest dinosaur discoveries, with remains first discovered in the late 1700s in the Netherlands. The fossilized bones, found in a subterranean quarry, were initially thought to be those of a prehistoric crocodile or perhaps even a whale. It took nearly forty years before scientists settled on its official name: *Mosasaurus*. It earned its name thanks to its discovery near the Meuse River, which was likely its home sixty-six to eighty million years ago, during the late Cretaceous Period. Despite its name, *Mosasaurus* is not technically a dinosaur but an aquatic or marine reptile. Its closest modern relative is the Komodo dragon. Growing to a length of more than seventy-one feet, *Mosasaurus* weighs in at a staggering twenty-nine metric tons. Today, *Mosasaurus* is one of Jurassic World's undisputed stars, living within its own aquatic habitat at the center of the main park where no visitor can miss it or one of its regularly scheduled feedings.

LENGTH
21.9M (71.8 ft)

HEIGHT
1.88M (6.16 ft)

WEIGHT
29 tonnes (64,000 lbs)

THE SPLASH ZONE

Inspired by one of Jurassic World's most popular attractions, The Splash Zone is the perfect drink to cool you down on a hot day . . . no poncho required.

YIELD: 1 DRINK

FOR THE GINGER SYRUP:

1 cup sugar

1 cup water

2- to 3-inch piece of ginger, peeled and cut into chunks

3 tablespoons dried butterfly pea flowers

FOR THE SPLASH ZONE:

4 to 5 large marshmallows

Ice

3 tablespoons ginger syrup

½ teaspoon vanilla bean paste

About 8 ounces soda water

TO SERVE:

Gummy shark or fish, optional

Wooden skewer, optional

SPECIAL SUPPLIES:

Kitchen shears

TO MAKE THE GINGER SYRUP

1. In a small saucepan over medium-high heat, bring the sugar, water, and ginger to a boil, stirring until sugar is dissolved, about 3 minutes.
2. Remove the pan from the heat, and add the flowers. Allow flowers to steep until the syrup is cooled completely, about 1 hour. Strain the syrup to remove flowers and ginger. Store the syrup in an airtight container in the refrigerator for up to 1 week.

TO MAKE THE SPLASH ZONE

3. Use the kitchen shears or a sharp knife to cut each marshmallow in half diagonally through the tall side. This will create two "teeth" from each marshmallow. Snip or cut a slit horizontally into the flat bottom of each tooth, so it can rest on the edge of the glass.
4. Fill a tall glass most of the way with crushed ice, and place the marshmallow teeth all around the edge, facing inward. Add the ginger syrup and vanilla paste to the glass, stir gently, and top off with soda water
5. If using the skewer, stick the gummy shark on one end and place in the glass so the shark is suspended above the jaws.

JURASSIC LAGOON CRAB CAKES

No visit to the Jurassic World Lagoon would be complete without a taste of our famous crab cakes. Unlike traditional New England or Maryland crab cakes, our version incorporates fresh corn and hot sauce for an enticing regional take on this classic starter.

YIELD: ABOUT 12 CRAB CAKES

FOR THE CRAB CAKES:
2 ears of corn, shucked
2 teaspoons vegetable oil or oil of choice
1 pound fresh crab meat
2 eggs, lightly beaten
1 tablespoon hot sauce
¼ cup mayonnaise
¼ cup thinly sliced green onions (about 4 green onions)
¼ cup bread crumbs

FOR THE BREADING:
1¼ cups bread crumbs
¼ cup cornmeal
6 tablespoons butter, melted, divided

FOR THE SAUCE:
½ cup mayonnaise
1 tablespoon hot sauce
Juice of ½ lemon
1 tablespoon chopped fresh parsley
Fresh ground black pepper, to taste

SPECIAL SUPPLIES:
Pastry brush

TO ROAST THE CORN:

1. Preheat the oven to 400°F.
2. Place the shucked corn on a baking sheet and rub with the oil. Roast the corn for 25 to 30 minutes, until tender and browned, turning them over halfway through cooking. Once cooked, remove from the oven, and let cool completely.
3. Working over a shallow bowl, place each ear of corn, tip-side down, in the bowl. Using the stalk as a handle, cut the kernels away from the cob into the bowl.

TO MAKE THE CRAB CAKES:

4. Prepare the crab meat by picking through it to remove any shells and breaking up the larger pieces.
5. In a large bowl, combine the eggs, hot sauce, mayonnaise, green onion, and 1 cup roasted corn kernels. Add in the crab meat and ¼ cup bread crumbs, and mix until combined.
6. Line a cookie sheet with a baking mat or parchment paper. Prepare the breading by mixing together the remaining 1¼ cup bread crumbs, cornmeal, and 2 tablespoons of butter together in a shallow bowl. Using a 2½-inch cookie scoop or measuring cup, scoop up a large ball of the crab mixture, and use your hands to gently form it into a patty. Gently press the patty into the bread crumb mixture on both sides to ensure it's evenly coated, and place on the cookie sheet. Repeat until all the crab mixture is gone, then transfer the sheet to the freezer, and freeze for 30 minutes.
7. Preheat the oven to 450°F. Using a pastry brush, butter a baking sheet with the melted butter and transfer the crab cakes to it. Brush the tops and sides of each cake with the remaining melted butter. Bake for 12 to 15 minutes, until golden brown.

TO MAKE THE SAUCE:

8. In a small bowl, whisk together all the ingredients.
9. Serve crab cakes warm with sauce on the side.

DON'T MISS

Underwater Observatory and Mosasaurus Feeding Show

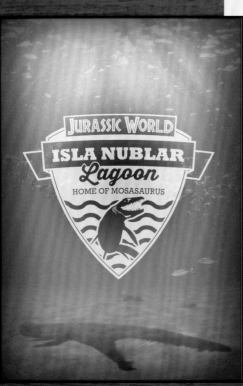

The centerpiece of the park's visitor experience, Jurassic World Lagoon attracts thousands of people who come to watch one of the island's most fearsome inhabitants in action. A specially designed underwater habitat is home to *Mosasaurus*. Park guests can observe this fascinating creature during feedings scheduled throughout the day. Viewing stands around the lagoon's edge offer spectacular views as a large shark such as a great white is suspended over the lagoon for *Mosasaurus* to consume. Those sitting close enough to the edge of the water risk being drenched as the enormous reptile makes quite the splash.

Also accessible is the Underwater Observatory, where visitors receive an unmatched "fish-eye" view of the lagoon's carefully monitored environment. Nothing compares to watching *Mosasaurus* feeding mere meters away from your seat! A separate aquarium serves as home to other aquatic dinosaur life re-created in the park's laboratories.

FEEDINGS DAILY AT 11AM AND 4PM

COCONUT PRAWNS

A mouthwatering snack found in the eateries near the Underwater Observatory, our Coconut Prawns takes inspiration from the cuisine of our Costa Rican neighbors. The recipe features a subtle blend of seasonings for preparing the shrimp.

YIELD: 6 SERVINGS

FOR THE COCONUT SAUCE:
½ cup full-fat coconut milk, stirred well
½ cup pepper jelly
1 teaspoon rice wine vinegar
½ teaspoon salt
1 teaspoon red curry powder
Juice of 1 lime

FOR THE COCONUT SHRIMP:
¼ cup prepared coconut sauce, plus more for dipping
Juice from ½ lemon
1 pound jumbo shrimp, approximately 15 count, peeled and deveined, tails left on
½ cup all-purpose flour
1 teaspoon sea salt
½ teaspoon baking powder
⅔ cup soda water
1 cup unsweetened, shredded coconut
1 cup panko bread crumbs
About 2 quarts of oil for frying, such as canola or safflower

SPECIAL SUPPLIES:
Fry thermometer

TIP:
Be sure to observe safe practices while frying. Don't forget your fry thermometer!

TO MAKE THE SAUCE:

1. Combine all the ingredients in a small saucepan over medium-high heat. Bring to a boil, stirring occasionally, then reduce heat to medium and simmer for 5 minutes, or until it coats the back of a spoon. Remove from heat and allow to cool before using as a marinade, around 30 minutes.

TO MAKE THE PRAWNS:

2. In a large bowl, combine ¼ cup of the prepared coconut sauce with the lemon juice. Add the shrimp, stirring to coat, and marinate in the refrigerator for 30 minutes.

3. In a separate large bowl, combine the flour, salt, baking powder, and soda water. Stir until just combined (it's okay if there are some lumps). Remove the shrimp from the marinade, discarding the excess, and gently mix it into the batter. Let stand at room temperature until ready to fry.

4. Combine the coconut and panko breadcrumbs in a shallow dish or pie plate to create the breading.

5. Add oil to a large high-sided skillet or Dutch oven fitted with a candy thermometer. Bring the oil up to temperature, between 365 and 375°F.

6. Pull each shrimp out of the batter and dip it in the breading, pressing to adhere the coconut and panko. Working in small batches, fry the shrimp until golden brown, about 1 minute per side, being careful not to overcrowd the pan. Remove from the pan and transfer to a plate lined with paper towels and sprinkle with salt.

7. Serve immediately with sauce for dipping.

BLACK COD WITH MISO AND COCONUT RICE

For many years, Jurassic World's famous Chilean Sea Bass—rumored to be based on a dish from the proposed menu for John Hammond's original Jurassic Park—was one of the most popular entrées served on the island. When the Chilean Sea Bass became endangered, our chefs adjusted the recipe to feature the more sustainable, but equally tasty, black cod instead. Served with coconut rice, this delectable fish dish adapts well to home cooking and is the perfect entrée for a slightly elevated weekend meal.

YIELD: 4 SERVINGS

FOR THE FISH:
⅓ cup red miso
¼ cup mirin
2 tablespoons rice wine vinegar
1 tablespoon toasted sesame oil
1 teaspoon ground ginger
Juice of 1 lime
1½ pounds skinless black cod, cut into 4 fillets
Vegetable oil, for baking sheet

FOR THE RICE:
1 cup water
1 cup lite coconut milk
½ teaspoon salt
1 cup rice

FOR THE GARNISH:
About ¼ cup vegetable oil
2 carrots, peeled into wide ribbons
4 green onions, sliced, white and light green parts only

1. Combine the red miso, mirin, rice wine vinegar, sesame oil, ground ginger, and lime juice in a shallow glass dish. Add the fish, turning to coat. Let stand at room temperature for 30 minutes.
2. While the fish is marinating, prepare the rice and garnish. For the rice, combine the water, coconut milk, and salt in a small saucepan over medium-high heat. Bring to a boil and add rice. Give the rice a quick stir, and reduce the heat to a simmer. Simmer rice for 20 minutes, uncovered, then remove from the heat. Fluff with a fork, and let stand, covered, for 5 more minutes.
3. For the garnish, heat ½ inch vegetable oil in a large skillet over medium-high heat. Add carrots, in batches if necessary, to the oil and fry for 2 to 3 minutes or until crisp. Drain on a paper towel, then toss with the green onion while still warm.
4. Line a rimmed baking sheet with foil and brush lightly with oil. Preheat broiler on low. Remove the fish from the marinade, and place on the lined baking sheet. Pour the marinade over the fish. Broil for around 6 minutes or until the fish is flaky and browned in spots.
5. To serve, divide the rice equally among four bowls. Place a fillet on top, and garnish with the carrot and green onion.

SEA FOAM

Isla Nublar was selected as the home for Jurassic World partially because of its tropical and subtropical climate, which is comparable to the climate scientists believe was prevalent during the time of the dinosaurs. While our star attractions are always quite comfortable, there are days when it gets pretty sultry for our human guests and staff. Luckily, we've got a variety of refreshing drinks to help you cool things down. Up your beverage game with this foamy, refreshing matcha drink—the perfect thirst quencher for a hot summer day.

YIELD: 2 DRINKS

FOR THE WHIPPED CREAM:
6 tablespoons heavy cream
1 tablespoon powdered sugar
1 teaspoon vanilla bean paste

FOR THE SEA FOAM:
1 cup pineapple juice
½ teaspoon unsweetened matcha powder
Ice
About 4 ounces soda water
Pineapple chunks, for garnish (optional)

TO MAKE THE WHIPPED CREAM:

1. Combine the heavy cream, sugar, and vanilla in a medium bowl, and whip until soft peaks form. Set aside.

TO MAKE THE SEA FOAM:

2. In a small bowl or measuring cup, whisk together the pineapple juice and matcha powder, until well blended.
3. To assemble, fill 2 tall glasses with ice and split the matcha juice between them. Top off with soda water, a dollop of whipped cream, and pineapple chunks, if using. Stir and enjoy immediately.

Flavors of Central America
from the Cretaceous Cruise

A journey through the heart of Isla Nublar awaits visitors who choose to undertake our Cretaceous Cruise. This guided tour of the island's interior dinosaur paddocks allows guests to experience the wonders of these majestic creatures, including *Stegosaurus*, *Stygimoloch*, *Baryonyx*, and *Hadrosaurus*. This particular area of the park bears the unmistakable influence of Central America, also found in the rich, flavorful dishes served here. They're inspired by centuries of culture and tradition, but always feature our unique Jurassic World twist.

THE OMNIVORE'S BOWL

Similar to chifrijo, a Costa Rican specialty, our Omnivore's Bowl includes a little bit of everything: beans, avocado, cheese, pico de gallo, and chicharrones (pork rinds) served on the side. You can substitute with corn chips if you want, but what true omnivore would?

YIELD: 6 TO 8 SERVINGS

FOR THE PICO DE GALLO:
4 ripe Roma tomatoes, chopped
3 tablespoons olive oil
1 tablespoon rice wine vinegar
½ teaspoon salt, or to taste
¼ cup roughly chopped cilantro leaves
1 small mango, diced

FOR THE BEANS:
1 tablespoon oil
1 tablespoon butter
1 yellow onion, diced, divided
¼ teaspoon ground coriander
½ teaspoon chili powder
1 teaspoon salt
One 15-ounce can whole pinto beans

TO SERVE:
1 cup Cotija or feta cheese
1 ripe avocado, diced
Chicharrones (pork rinds) or corn chips

TO MAKE THE PICO DE GALLO:

1. Combine all the ingredients for the pico de gallo in a medium bowl, plus half the diced onion from the ingredients list for the beans. Set aside until ready to serve. This salsa is best if it is made fresh.

TO MAKE THE BEANS:

2. In a large skillet, melt the butter in the oil over medium-high heat. Add the remaining half of the onion, and cook until translucent and extremely soft, 3 to 5 minutes. Add the spices and salt, stir, and cook 2 to 3 minutes more.

3. Add the beans with their liquid to the pan and bring to a simmer. Simmer for 5 to 8 minutes, until most of the liquid is absorbed. Remove the pan from the heat, and smash the beans with a fork or the back of a spoon directly in the pan, leaving some chunks.

TO ASSEMBLE:

4. Add the beans to your serving dish, spreading them in a thick layer in the bottom of the dish. Sprinkle with Cotija cheese.

5. Using a slotted spoon, layer the pico de gallo over the cheese and beans. Sprinkle the avocado on top and serve with chicharrones or chips on the side.

CHORREADAS DE NUBLAR

If you've never had chorreadas—Costa Rican pancakes prepared with fresh corn—you're in for a real treat with this sweet recipe! In the park, we serve our version of this traditional dish with honey and crème fraîche, but feel free to mix it up at home with whatever toppings you want.

YIELD: ABOUT 8 PANCAKES

5 ears of corn, shucked

½ cup packed light brown sugar

¼ cup flour

2 eggs

¼ cup milk

2 tablespoons butter, melted, plus more for the pan

Crème fraîche, to serve (optional)

Honey, to serve (optional)

TO MAKE THE ROASTED CORN:

1. Preheat the oven to 400°F.
2. Place the shucked corn on a cookie sheet. Roast the corn for 20 to 30 minutes, turning halfway through, or until tender and golden brown in some spots. Some char is okay, too. Remove from oven and let cool, until no longer hot to the touch.
3. Working over a shallow bowl, place each ear of corn, tip-side down, in the bowl. Using the stalk as a handle, cut the kernels away from the cob into the bowl.

TO MAKE THE CHORREADAS:

4. Combine 2 cups of the roasted corn kernels with the light brown sugar, flour, eggs, milk, and 2 tablespoons of melted butter in the bowl of a food processor or blender, and blend until a batter comes together. Be careful not to over-blend; there should still be chunks of corn throughout.
5. Heat a large skillet over medium heat. Melt a small pat of butter in the skillet, and add ¼ cup scoop of the batter. Let the cake cook until most of the bubbles have risen and popped, about 3 minutes, then flip and cook the other side until golden brown, another 2 to 3 minutes.
6. Serve with crème fraîche, honey, or both.

TIP:

If fresh corn is not in season, frozen corn will work fine. Cook the corn according to the package directions, drain, and spread it out on a cookie sheet. Roast for 5 to 10 minutes, or until fragrant and golden brown.

TIP:

For a savory variation, reduce the brown sugar to 2 tablespoons and add a diced jalapeño or 1 tablespoon snipped chives to the batter.

FIELD GUIDE:
STEGOSAURUS

Though it might look scary with its long, spiked tail and massive, bony plates set into its back, *Stegosaurus* is actually not very aggressive unless provoked. It originally went extinct during the late Jurassic Period, with the first specimens found in the 1870s near Morrison, Colorado. As park visitors observe, this dinosaur grows to an average length of over thirty feet, weighs in between three and four metric tons, and can swing its tail with tremendous force when needed to defend itself. An herbivore, its diet consists of whatever low-lying plants it happens across. Park visitors can discover several *Stegosauruses* along the Cretaceous Cruise and wandering Gyrosphere Valley, while younger *Stegosauruses* can be visited at the Gentle Giants Petting Zoo.

--- FOOTPRINT ---

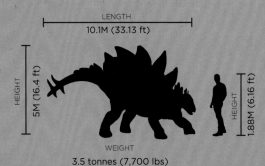

LENGTH
10.1M (33.13 ft)

HEIGHT
5M (16.4 ft)

HEIGHT
1.88M (6.16 ft)

WEIGHT
3.5 tonnes (7,700 lbs)

RAPTOR PACK FRESCAS

Based on a classic agua fresca, a popular drink in Mexico, our Raptor Pack Frescas (pictured on pages 80 to 81) can be made with nearly any fruit combination. We offer variations inspired by each of the animals in Jurassic World's fearsome raptor pack: Charlie, Delta, Echo, and of course, Blue, the leader and most intelligent raptor ever created at Jurassic World.

YIELD: 2 DRINKS FOR EACH FLAVOR

FOR BLUE'S FRESCA (BLUEBERRY GINGER):

1 cup water

2 tablespoons cane sugar

2 tablespoons blueberries

1 tablespoon butterfly pea flower, dried

One 4-inch piece of ginger, peeled and sliced thin

Crushed ice

FOR CHARLIE'S FRESCA (CUCUMBER MINT):

1 cup water

2 tablespoons cane sugar

2 large sprigs of mint

Peels from 1 large or 2 small cucumbers

Juice of 1 lime

1½ cups seeded and diced cucumber, divided

BLUE'S FRESCA

1. In a small saucepan over medium-high heat, combine the water, sugar, blueberries, butterfly pea flower, and ginger. Bring to a boil and cook, stirring to dissolve the sugar, for five minutes. Remove the pan from heat and allow to cool completely. Strain, but do not discard blueberries or ginger.
2. Once the syrup is cooled, pour it into a blender, along with the strained blueberries, and one piece of ginger from the syrup. Puree until smooth.
3. Fill two glasses with crushed ice, and pour the aqua fresca over the top. Stir and serve with a boba straw.

CHARLIE'S FRESCA

1. In a small saucepan over medium-high heat, combine the water, sugar, mint, and cucumber peel. Bring to a boil, stirring to dissolve the sugar. Remove the pan from the heat as soon as the sugar is dissolved. Allow to cool completely, and then strain.
2. Once the syrup is cooled, pour it into a blender, add the lime juice, and 1 cup of the chopped cucumber. Puree until smooth.
3. Dice the remaining ½ cup of cucumber small enough to fit through a boba straw. Split the diced cucumber between 2 glasses, fill with crushed ice, and pour the aqua fresca over the top. Stir and serve with a boba straw.

SECRET MENU

What's better than a cool drink on a hot day? Popsicles! Use popsicle molds to turn any of the Raptor Pack Frescas into a refreshing frozen treat.

FOR DELTA'S FRESCA (STRAWBERRY HIBISCUS):

1 cup water

2 tablespoons cane sugar

2 tablespoons dried hibiscus flower or one hibiscus tea bag

Juice of 1 lime

1½ cups diced strawberries, divided

Crushed ice

DELTA'S FRESCA

1. In a small saucepan over medium-high heat, combine the water, sugar, and hibiscus. Bring to a boil, stirring to dissolve the sugar. Remove the pan from the heat as soon as the sugar is dissolved. Allow to cool completely, and then strain, reserving 1 hibiscus flower, if using for garnish.
2. Once the syrup is cooled, pour it into a blender, add the lime juice, and 1 cup of the chopped strawberries. Puree until smooth.
3. Dice the remaining ½ cup of strawberries small enough to fit through a boba straw. Split the diced fruit between 2 glasses, fill with crushed ice, and pour the aqua fresca over the top. Stir and serve with a boba straw.

FOR ECHO'S FRESCA (PINEAPPLE LIME):

1 cup water

2 tablespoons cane sugar

Zest and juice of 1 lime

1½ cups diced pineapple, divided

Crushed ice

ECHO'S FRESCA

1. In a small saucepan over medium-high heat, combine the water, sugar, and lime zest. Bring to a boil, stirring to dissolve the sugar. Remove the pan from the heat as soon as the sugar is dissolved. Allow to cool completely.
2. Once the syrup is cooled, pour it into a blender, add the lime juice, and 1 cup of the chopped pineapple. Puree until smooth.
3. Dice the remaining ½ cup of pineapple small enough to fit through a boba straw. Split the diced fruit between 2 glasses, fill with crushed ice, and pour the aqua fresca over the top. Stir and serve with a boba straw.

AGUA DE AVIARY

A variation on a popular Costa Rican blend of ginger and lime, our Agua de Aviary is an easily prepared refreshment that's a perfect thirst quencher on a warm summer day. In Jurassic World, you'll find it's a preferred choice for guests of all ages who find their way to our Aviary's observation deck. It's also the key ingredient in our Avian Escape cocktail (page 135), which adds a little something extra for those who like their drinks with some bite.

YIELD: EIGHT 12-OUNCE SERVINGS

2 cups cane sugar or turbinado sugar
6 ounces ginger, peeled and chopped
1 cinnamon stick
12 cups water
1 cup fresh-squeezed lime juice (from about 6 limes)
Limes for garnish, optional

1. Combine the sugar, ginger, cinnamon, and water in a large pot over medium-high heat. Bring to a boil, and then reduce to a simmer, stirring to dissolve the sugar. Simmer for 10 minutes, and then remove the pot from the heat. Allow syrup to cool completely.
2. Once the syrup has cooled, strain into a large pitcher, add lime juice, cover, and refrigerate to chill. Serve chilled over ice. Garnish with limes as desired.

DON'T MISS

Cretaceous Cruise

Eager visitors will surely want to experience the Cretaceous Cruise, Jurassic World's one-of-a-kind guided tour through several of Isla Nublar's larger dinosaur habitats. Each guest paddles his or her own kayak, following one of our experienced guides into this wondrous inner sanctum. Be sure to allot several hours for this part of your visit to the park. You'll navigate a slow-moving river on a route that will immerse you in an environment teeming with dinosaurs like the *Apatosaurus*, *Baryonyx*, *Stegosaurus*, and nearly one hundred other species, as well as other dynamic animal and plant life. Much of the flora you'll see on your tour is cultivated in our Botanical Gardens, which provides a variety of foods for the herbivores living in the park. One of the key stops along the cruise is the Jurassic World Aviary, home to our *Pteranodons* and *Dimorphodons*.

THE PATIENT PREDATOR BOWL

Inspired by carne mechada, a popular dish in Venezuela, our take on this tangy mix of shredded beef and vegetables cooked in a fragrant blend of spices is named for one of Jurassic World's formidable carnivores: *Baryonyx*. *Baryonyx*'s hunting style is different than the other big carnivores. Instead of hunting openly, it patiently lies in wait for its prey, choosing the right moment to strike. For you to enjoy this hearty dish, you will have to exercise similar patience. While many recipes call for a pressure cooker, our version works best when employing a Dutch oven. The slow-cooked result is mouthwatering and absolutely worth the wait.

YIELD: 6 TO 8 SERVINGS

2½ to 3 pounds brisket

1½ teaspoons kosher salt, divided

2 tablespoons oil

1 large onion, diced

2 carrots, scrubbed and cut into 2- to 3-inch chunks

1 parsnip, scrubbed and cut into 2- to 3-inch chunks

6 sprigs of cilantro tied in a bunch with cotton cooking twine

2 bay leaves

½ teaspoon dried thyme

1 teaspoon dried oregano

½ teaspoon cumin

½ teaspoon paprika

2 tablespoons Worcestershire sauce

4+ cups water

2 cups white rice

Cilantro, for garnish

Chopped white onion, for garnish

1. Rub the brisket on both sides with 1 teaspoon of salt and set aside.

2. Heat a Dutch oven or large pot over medium-high heat and add the oil and onions. Sauté the onions for 3 to 5 minutes, until translucent. Push the onions to the sides of the pot to make a space in the middle for the meat.

3. Add the brisket to the Dutch oven, and brown for 3 to 5 minutes on each side, stirring the onions a bit as you're cooking so they brown but do not burn. Add in the carrots, parsnip, cilantro, spices, remaining ½ teaspoon of salt, Worcestershire sauce, and water, making sure the meat is covered. Bring to a boil, and then cover and reduce to a simmer. Cook on low, covered, for 2½ to 3 hours, until the brisket is tender and falling apart.

4. When the brisket is done, turn off the heat, and use tongs to remove the brisket to a cutting board. Discard the bay leaves and cilantro. Remove the carrots and parsnip chunks to a separate cutting board, and finely chop.

5. Ladle 2 cups of broth into a large saucepan over medium-high heat. Add 2 cups of water and rice. Bring to a boil, cover, and reduce the heat to low so the rice is just simmering. After 8 minutes, add the chopped vegetables, stir, cover, and continue to simmer for 10 to 15 minutes more, or until the rice is tender. Remove from heat and fluff the rice with a fork.

6. While the rice is cooking, shred the beef using a carving knife and fork, discarding any fat, and return to the Dutch oven. Cover until ready to serve.

7. Serve the beef over the rice, garnished with chopped cilantro or chopped white onion.

FIELD GUIDE:
BARYONYX

One of the first species re-created by InGen scientists, *Baryonyx* is a dinosaur you wouldn't want to meet in the wild, but it's a fascinating and impressive creature to observe in the park. It's an amphibian, thriving on land as well as in water. Based on available evidence, *Baryonyx* roamed the rivers and lakes of Europe and northern Africa 125 to 130 million years ago. As is often true in this field, the first remains were discovered by accident, in this case by an amateur fossil hunter in 1983 near Surrey, England. Growing to an average length of thirty feet and weighing more than three thousand pounds, it can move through water or over land at speeds impressive for its size. Its diet consists largely of fish, small dinosaurs, and whatever other animals might stray too close to the water's edge. Like its modern-day cousin, the crocodile, it is content to lie in wait for hours, or even days sometimes, until its next meal crosses its path. Guests at Jurassic World stand a good chance of seeing a *Baryonyx* along one of the riverbanks during the Cretaceous Cruise.

--- FOOTPRINT ---

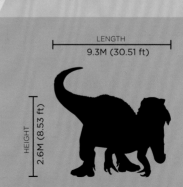

LENGTH
9.3M (30.51 ft)

HEIGHT
2.6M (8.53 ft)

HEIGHT
1.88M (6.16 ft)

WEIGHT
1.7 tonnes (3,770 lbs)

ISLA ICE

Isla Ice is Jurassic World's take on copo, a traditional Costa Rican iced dessert usually sold by street vendors, or at small stands by the beach. Our take on this local favorite uses a strawberry granita as the base, meaning you don't have to have a shaved-ice maker to enjoy this delicious treat at home.

YIELD: 6 TO 8 SERVINGS

FOR THE GRANITA:

2 cups strawberries, rinsed and stemmed, plus more for garnish if desired

½ cup sugar

Juice of 1 lime

1 cup water

FOR THE COPO:

One 14-ounce can sweetened condensed milk, divided

About ½ cup malted milk powder, divided

1 carton vanilla ice cream

Strawberries, for garnish

SPECIAL SUPPLIES:

9-by-12-inch glass lasagna pan

Sundae glass (optional)

Small ice cream scoop

TO MAKE THE GRANITA:

1. Puree the strawberries and sugar in a blender or food processor until smooth. Add the strawberry puree, lime juice, and water to a saucepan over medium heat and bring to a simmer. Simmer for 3 to 5 minutes, or until the sugar is dissolved. Strain the syrup through a fine-mesh strainer into the lasagna pan, and transfer to the freezer for 1 hour.

2. Remove the pan from the freezer and scrape the granita with a fork, pulling the ice crystals from the bottom and sides. Return the pan to the freezer and continue to freeze for a total of 3 hours, scraping with a fork to collect ice crystals every 30 to 45 minutes. When the granita is done, transfer to an airtight container and store in the freezer until ready to use.

TO MAKE THE COPO:

3. Use a small ice cream scoop to place one scoop of strawberry granita in the bottom of a sundae glass or other tall glass. Drizzle 2 tablespoons of sweetened condensed milk on top, followed by a scoop of vanilla ice cream sprinkled with about 1 tablespoon malted milk powder. Continue to layer granita, condensed milk, ice cream, and malted milk powder until the glass is full, ending with vanilla ice cream and malted milk powder.

4. Garnish with whole strawberries if desired, and serve .

COCONUT FUDGE

Though it's not unique to the region, coconut fudge still has a special place in Costa Rican baking and snacking. The recipe for our coconut fudge—a popular "take-home" treat at the park—emulates several of the variations found throughout Central America. Anyone in your family who harbors a sweet tooth will surely thank you!

YIELD: ABOUT 30 CANDIES

4 tablespoons unsalted butter

One 14-ounce can sweetened condensed milk

2½ cups shredded unsweetened coconut, divided, pulsed in a food processor until it resembles small grains of rice

3 ounces gingersnap cookies, pulverized in a food processor

About 1 teaspoon black lava salt, flaky sea salt, or other finishing salt

SPECIAL SUPPLIES:

Flower-shaped cookie cutter

1. Line a 9-by-13-inch glass baking pan with parchment paper, and set aside.

2. In a medium, heavy-bottomed saucepan, heat the butter and sweetened condensed milk over medium heat, stirring occasionally, until the butter is melted. Add the coconut, reserving about a ½ cup. Stir until combined.

3. Remove the pan from heat, add the crushed gingersnaps, and stir them in until mostly incorporated. Return the pan to medium heat, and cook, stirring continuously, until the mixture is thick and begins to pull away from the sides and bottom of the pan, about 10 to 15 minutes. Pour mixture into the prepared pan, using a spatula to make sure it's spread evenly across the pan.

4. Chill the fudge in the refrigerator for 2 hours, and then use a flower-shaped cookie cutter to cut out the candies. Place the remaining coconut on a shallow plate and turn each candy in it to coat all sides. Use the tip of your pinkie to make a small indent in the center of each candy, and sprinkle a few grains of the salt in each.

TIP:

- Dipping the cookie cutter in powdered sugar between candies can help keep the cookie cutter from sticking.
- If you don't want to use a cookie cutter, the mixture can be hand-rolled, after chilling, into 2-inch balls. Roll the balls in coconut, and add a few grains of salt to the top of each one if desired.

FIELD GUIDE:
PTERANODON

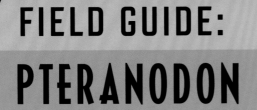

One of the largest flying reptiles, *Pteranodon* rules the Aviary at Jurassic World as it did the skies during the late Cretaceous Period, between eighty and eighty-five million years ago. Its technical classification is that of "pterosaur," meaning it's not actually a dinosaur. The first specimens were found in 1870 in western Kansas. Subsequent finds were excavated across the American Midwest, which millions of years ago was covered by the vast yet shallow Western Interior Seaway, which divided the North American continent. Though it is relatively short in stature, reaching an average length of just over seven feet, *Pteranodon*'s wingspan can reach up to twenty-five feet. It is a carnivore whose diet consisted of fish and smaller marine life despite the fact that it has no teeth. An elongated and very sharp beak and large claws are its primary defenses, and it tends to move and rest in groups. Guests can see these and some of the park's other winged residents by visiting the massive Aviary, which is one of several points of interest along the Cretaceous Cruise.

--- FOOTPRINT ---

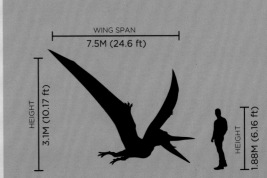

WING SPAN
7.5M (24.6 ft)

HEIGHT
3.1M (10.17 ft)

HEIGHT
1.88M (6.16 ft)

Snacks and sweets from the Gentle Giants Petting Zoo and beyond

When kids visit Jurassic World, they generally have one goal: explore the park until they drop. And we get it! There are so many things to do and too many dinosaurs to see in a single day. Somewhere along the way they're going to be hungry, and they won't want to wait while the grown-ups order that fancy steak or deconstructed salad. Something lighter to keep up their energy might be the way to go, and the same is definitely true at home. Here are some of our favorite recipes for fast, easy, and yummy snacks and sweets custom-made for the park's youngest guests.

CERATOPS PASTRY CRESTS

This delectable breakfast offering takes its name and shape from the series of horns along the edges of the distinctive frill on the back of *Sinoceratops*'s skull.

YIELD: 4 PASTRIES

FOR THE PASTRIES:
Juice of 1 lemon
1 tablespoon honey
1 tablespoon packed light brown sugar
½ teaspoon cinnamon
2 small apples, peeled, cored, and chopped
½ cup currants (reserve 8 for "the eyes")
1 package frozen puff pastry, defrosted
1 egg
1 tablespoon water

FOR THE CINNAMON SUGAR TOPPING:
1 tablespoon sugar
¼ teaspoon cinnamon

1. In a large bowl, combine the lemon juice, honey, brown sugar, cinnamon, chopped apples, and currants. Let the filling rest at room temperature while you prepare the dough to allow the apples to soften slightly.

2. Roll out each defrosted piece of puff pastry until it is large enough to cover a 10- to 12-inch dinner plate. Using a dinner plate as a template, cut one circle of dough out of each piece of puff pastry. Cut each circle in half and then in half again, forming 8 pie-shaped pieces. Reserve scraps.

3. Line a cookie sheet with a baking mat or parchment. Make an egg wash by whisking the egg with the water in a small bowl. Working on the prepared cookie sheet with one pair of triangles at a time, place a ¼ cup of the apple filling in the center of one triangle. Brush a little egg wash around the edge, and cover with the other triangle. Use a fork or your fingers to press the edges of the pastry together, sealing completely so that the filling doesn't spill out.

4. Cut 8 to 9 slits into the curved side of the triangle, twisting alternate tabs in opposite directions to create the spikes. About 2 inches down from the spikes, cut two holes, about an inch long, in the center of the top crust of the pastry to form the Sino's distinctive crest. Brush the whole pastry with egg wash. Repeat with the remaining triangles until you have four pastry dinosaurs.

5. Use the leftover scraps of pastry to make four small horns, one for each *Sinoceratop*s. Using more egg wash, secure the horns in place, about a ½ inch above the point of the triangle to form the *Sinoceratops*'s nose horn, arranging it so that it curls up toward the spikes. Place two currant "eyes" on either side of the horn, slightly above the point. At the point of the triangle, snip a slit and twist, curling up to form the beak-like mouth.

6. In a small bowl, mix the cinnamon and sugar. Sprinkle each pastry generously with the cinnamon-sugar mix. Chill pastries in the refrigerator for 30 minutes.

7. Preheat the oven to 400°F.

8. Bake the pastries in the oven for 20 to 25 minutes, until golden brown and crisp. Let them cool slightly before serving.

MARSHMALLOW EGG SURPRISE

From the mighty *Tyrannosaurus rex* to the pint-size *Compsognathus*, nearly all species of dinosaurs and marine reptiles laid eggs. At Jurassic World, our eggs are developed in the lab, but this egg-shaped rice cereal treat is developed in the kitchen. They're perfect for parties or other special occasions, and kids get a kick out of pulling these apart, especially once they discover there's a gummy surprise inside!

YIELD: ABOUT 1 DOZEN EGG SURPRISES

6 cups puffed rice cereal

3 tablespoons butter, plus more for greasing hands and egg molds

10 ounces marshmallows

4 ounces white chocolate, melted

Gummy dinosaurs or other candy creatures

Luster dust, optional

Popping candy, optional

SPECIAL SUPPLIES:

Large plastic eggs, about 4 inches long

1. Measure cereal into a large bowl and set aside. In a large microwave-safe bowl, combine 3 tablespoons of butter and the marshmallows. Microwave for 1 minute, remove, and stir until all the marshmallows and butter have melted. Stir the mixture into the cereal, and combine thoroughly. Allow to cool for 3 to 5 minutes. Have the extra butter (softened), plastic eggs, melted chocolate, and gummy dinosaurs ready.

2. When the mixture is cool enough to handle, grease the inside of both halves of a plastic egg. Working with one half at a time, press about a ½ cup of the cereal mixture into each half, shaping with your fingers until the mixture forms each half of an empty egg. The mixture should extend over the edges of the plastic egg halves a bit. Dip the exposed edge of one half of the treat into the white chocolate, insert a gummy dinosaur into the other half and press the two halves of the plastic egg together. Twist the halves back and forth to firmly join the two halves.

3. Let the egg set for 3 to 4 minutes, and then gently remove the plastic shells. Repeat until all the eggs are made. Once the eggs are set, lightly brush them with silver, blue, or green luster dust and dot them with popping candy, if desired.

PORTRAIT OF STIGGY TOAST

One of Jurassic World's more popular—and adorable—residents, *Stygimoloch*, or "Stiggy," is a dinosaur that kids will be looking for while taking the Cretaceous Cruise or a tour through Gyrosphere Valley. Her prominent spiked skull is unlike most of the park's other inhabitants, providing unique inspiration for this next-level breakfast treat.

YIELD: 2 SERVINGS

¼ cup peanut butter or preferred nut butter

½ tablespoon dark, unsweetened cocoa powder

1 tablespoon powdered sugar

1 red apple

1 teaspoon apple cider vinegar, to keep apple from browning

1 large strawberry, hulled

4 blueberries

2 pieces of bread, cut from a round loaf

1. Make the chocolate nut butter by mixing together the peanut butter, cocoa powder, and powdered sugar in a small bowl until smooth and well combined.
2. Making shallow cuts, remove two sides of the apple to form Stiggy's domed forehead. Core the rest of the apple and slice it into thin slices. Cut some of the slices in half to create Stiggy's shorter crown spikes.
3. Spread the nut butter on both pieces of toast, making it a little thicker toward the top where you will arrange the spikes. Place the apple dome on the middle third of the toast, and arrange apple spikes along the top edge.
4. Add two blueberries to each Stiggy for eyes. Cut the strawberry in half from tip to stem and place along the bottom of the toast to create her beak. Serve immediately.

SAUROPOD-FRIENDLY SNACKS

Sauropods—long-necked, four-legged dinosaurs like *Brachiosaurus* and *Apatosaurus*—love to eat their greens. When the veggies are presented the right way, kids can love them, too. These scrummy baked snacks are similar to traditional "tater tots" with one big difference: They're made of broccoli. Serve them warm with ranch dressing, Spicy Ketchup (page 49), or regular ketchup and you'll soon find your kids eating as many greens as the gentle dinosaurs for which these tasty tots are named.

YIELD: ABOUT 20 TOTS

16 ounces frozen broccoli, steamed

2 cloves garlic

1½ teaspoons salt

1 tablespoon butter, melted

¼ teaspoon paprika

¼ teaspoon ground black pepper

⅔ cup finely shredded cheddar cheese

⅔ cup panko bread crumbs

1. In the bowl of a food processor, pulse the broccoli and garlic until fine. Scrape down the sides of the bowl, add the spices, salt, and butter, and pulse 2 or 3 more times to combine. Add the cheese and panko, and pulse until just combined. Transfer the mixture to a bowl and chill in the refrigerator for at least 30 minutes.
2. Place a cookie sheet in the oven, and preheat both the oven and the sheet to 375°F. Line a separate cookie sheet with a piece of parchment paper to stage your tots.
3. Remove the broccoli mixture from the refrigerator. Scoop, with a cookie scoop or spoon about 2 tablespoons of the mixture and use your hands to form the mixture into 2- to 3-inch "tots" and place on the lined cookie sheet.
4. Once all the tots are shaped, pull the hot cookie sheet out of the oven and carefully slide the parchment paper with the tots onto it. Return to the oven and bake until the tots are golden brown on both sides, approximately 8 to 10 minutes, gently turning over the tots with a metal spatula or tongs halfway through.
5. Serve warm with Spicy Ketchup (page 49).

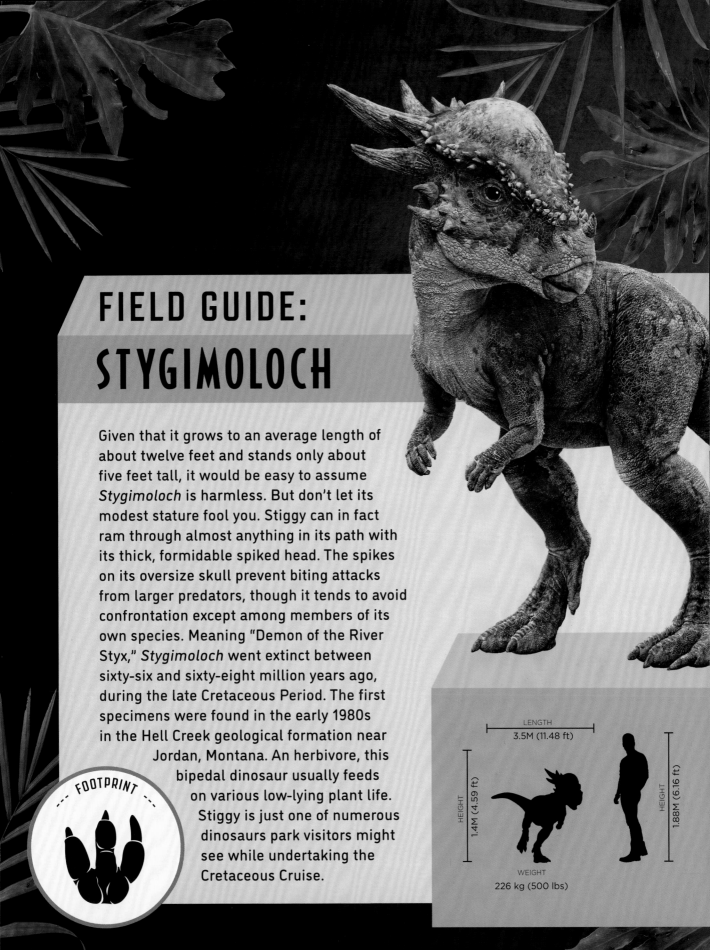

FIELD GUIDE:
STYGIMOLOCH

Given that it grows to an average length of about twelve feet and stands only about five feet tall, it would be easy to assume *Stygimoloch* is harmless. But don't let its modest stature fool you. Stiggy can in fact ram through almost anything in its path with its thick, formidable spiked head. The spikes on its oversize skull prevent biting attacks from larger predators, though it tends to avoid confrontation except among members of its own species. Meaning "Demon of the River Styx," *Stygimoloch* went extinct between sixty-six and sixty-eight million years ago, during the late Cretaceous Period. The first specimens were found in the early 1980s in the Hell Creek geological formation near Jordan, Montana. An herbivore, this bipedal dinosaur usually feeds on various low-lying plant life. Stiggy is just one of numerous dinosaurs park visitors might see while undertaking the Cretaceous Cruise.

--- FOOTPRINT ---

LENGTH
3.5M (11.48 ft)

HEIGHT
1.4M (4.59 ft)

HEIGHT
1.88M (6.16 ft)

WEIGHT
226 kg (500 lbs)

RAPTOR CLAW SCONES

Before Jurassic World, footprints left by dinosaurs were one of the richest sources of information pertaining to the movements and behavior of these amazing creatures. The oldest known fossilized prints date back 240 million years—to the very beginning of the dinosaur age. Inspired by the casts made of prominent fossilized *Velociraptor* footprints found in Outer Mongolia, our Raptor Claw scones are a tasty, sweet and salty treat.

YIELD: 8 SCONES

½ cup whole raw cashews

2 cups all-purpose flour

⅓ cup sugar

1 tablespoon baking powder

1 teaspoon kosher salt

6 tablespoons unsalted butter, frozen for 5 minutes

½ cup chocolate chunks or chips

½ sweetened shredded coconut

1 egg

½ cup heavy cream

FIELD GUIDE:

Before Jurassic World, paleontologists would measure the size and the distance between a dinosaur's prints to gauge how fast the dinosaur walked or ran, based on knowledge of a particular specimen's estimated size.

1. Preheat the oven to 425°F. Prepare two baking sheets by lining them with parchment paper or a silicone baking mat.
2. Sort through the cashews and select 24 to serve as the "claws" on the scone. Place the 24 in a small bowl and store in the freezer until needed. Roughly chop the remaining cashews and set aside.
3. In a large bowl, mix the flour, sugar, baking powder, and salt until well combined. Cut the cold butter into small pieces and add to the dry mixture. With a pastry cutter or two forks, cut the butter into the flour mixture until all the butter is pea-size or smaller. Add the chopped cashews, chocolate, and coconut, and stir gently to combine.
4. In a small bowl or measuring cup, whisk the egg into the heavy cream. Add the egg mixture to the dry ingredients, and mix them together until a shaggy dough forms. Reserve the bowl you mixed the egg and cream in for use later in the recipe.
5. Knead the dough gently in the bowl until it comes together. Transfer the dough onto one of the prepared baking sheets and pat out into a 1½- to 2-inch-thick circle. Brush the dough with the leftover cream from the small bowl. Cut the circle into eighths to form triangles or wedges.
6. Move 4 of the scones to the second prepared baking sheet. Make sure the scones on each sheet are spaced well apart. Cut two slits vertically into the curved side of the wedges, one slightly shorter than the other, about 1½ to 2 inches long. Spread apart the "toes" and insert 1 cashew "claw" into each toe, 3 for each scone.
7. Chill both sheets for 10 minutes in the refrigerator and then bake 10 to 12 minutes until golden brown. Allow to cool on the sheet for at least 10 minutes. Serve warm or at room temperature. Store in an airtight container for 1 to 2 days.

AMBER LOLLIPOPS

As you know from the "Mr. DNA" show at the Innovation Center, the key to creating genetically engineered dinosaurs is DNA found in the blood of mosquitos preserved in amber. That single important discovery evolved into the thrilling park called Jurassic World. This candy treat is inspired by those precious amber fossils, with sesame seeds to represent the prehistoric mosquito trapped in the sap.

YIELD: ABOUT 16 POPS

½ cup water

1 cup sugar

6 tablespoons dark corn syrup

½ tablespoon butter

¼ teaspoon orange oil, not extract

1 tablespoon seeds, such as black sesame, toasted sesame, anise, or poppy

SPECIAL SUPPLIES:

About 16 lollipop sticks

Candy thermometer

Baking mat

Cellophane treat bags

1. Bring the water to a boil in a medium heavy-bottomed saucepan. Remove from the heat, and add sugar, corn syrup, and butter. Return the pan to low heat and stir gently until the sugar is dissolved. Warm the candy thermometer under hot water and attach it to the side of the pan without letting it touch the bottom. Raise the heat to high, and continue to cook, until the temperature reaches 300°F, about 10 to 15 minutes. It is important not to leave sugar unattended and to closely monitor the thermometer. Remove from the heat and stir in the orange oil. Leave the pan off the heat and allow to cool to 240°F.

2. While the sugar is cooling, set up a baking mat with lollipop sticks, placed 2 to 3 inches apart. Sprinkle a small cluster of seeds at the top of each stick. When the mixture has cooled to 240°F, use a metal spoon to carefully drop about 1 tablespoon of syrup onto the top of each stick, letting it pool into a lollipop shape. If the mixture becomes too stiff, gently warm it on the stove to bring it back up to temperature.

3. Let the candy set 10 to 15 minutes and then wrap in cellophane treat bags or store in an airtight container, in layers separated by parchment for 3 to 5 days.

HYDRATION POPS

Our version of this popular and easy-to-make treat features a regional twist: coconut water. Coconut water is packed with electrolytes, making it a healthy alternative to many sports drinks. Combine with fresh fruits, such as strawberries, peaches, or pineapple, and you're set for those hot, humid days spent exploring the dinosaurs' habitats . . . or sitting by the pool.

YIELD: ABOUT 4 POPSICLES OF EACH FLAVOR

FOR THE STRAWBERRY POPSICLE:
1 cup chopped strawberries, from about 2 cups of berries
1 cup coconut water
2 tablespoons honey

FOR THE PEACH POPSICLE:
1 cup peach chunks, from about 2 peaches
1 cup coconut water
2 tablespoons honey

FOR THE PINEAPPLE-COCONUT POPSICLE:
1 cup coconut water
½ cup coconut juice or lite coconut milk
½ cup pineapple juice or crushed pineapple

SPECIAL SUPPLIES:
4-ounce popsicle molds

1. Puree in a blender the fruit or juice for whichever flavor popsicle you are making with the coconut water and honey, if using, until most of the fruit chunks are gone (some small pieces are okay). Fill the popsicle molds, and freeze until solid, about 6 to 8 hours. To help disperse fruit you may want to stir or shake the molds.
2. Serve straight from the freezer for a cool, fruity treat on a hot day.

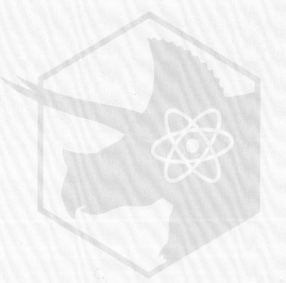

DON'T MISS

Innovation Center

For first-time visitors to Jurassic World and even for returning guests, the park's Innovation Center is a must-visit. Here you'll learn the history of the island and the park along with the original research and exploration that resulted in the creation of all our dinosaurs. Experience each of the park's assets via holograms in our Holoscape—just one of more than one hundred interactive exhibits that provide guests with a crash course in the science and craft of genetically engineering dinosaurs. Younger visitors might want to try their hand at digging for dinosaur fossils in our special hands-on dig site. Maybe they'll find their own fossil of a claw or massive tooth! You can also watch some of our scientists in action in the Innovation Center's Hammond Creation Lab. In it's lab—named for Dr. John Hammond, the man who first conceived of Jurassic World, it's in this lab that new dinosaur specimens are cloned, hatched, and added to the park every year!

DNA EXCAVATION -ZONE-

POPCORN TAIL CLUBS

The name and shape of these fun snacks is a tribute to *Ankylosaurus* and the prominent club on the end of its tail, which it uses to defend itself against predators. Easy to enjoy while on the move, these sweets are a popular treat with children exploring Jurassic World.

YIELD: ABOUT 16 SERVINGS

20 cups of popped popcorn, about ¾ cup of kernels

¼ cup butter, plus more for greasing hands

1 cup light corn syrup

1 cup mini marshmallows

2 cups powdered sugar

1 tablespoon cocoa powder

½ teaspoon salt

1 tablespoon water

2 drops green food coloring

2 packages green popping candy, optional

SPECIAL SUPPLIES:

18 to 20 lollipop sticks

Cellophane treat bags, optional

1. Prepare a cookie sheet by lining with it with parchment paper. Have the popcorn in a large bowl, and the extra butter for greasing your hands close by.
2. Combine all the ingredients, except the popcorn and popping candy, in a medium saucepan, over medium-high heat. Bring to a boil, stirring continuously, until all the marshmallows are melted and the mixture is smooth. Remove from the heat and pour over the popcorn, stirring quickly to combine.
3. Using buttered hands, shape a narrow stem of popcorn around the top of a lollipop stick. Form two small popcorn balls, about a ¼ cup each, and press them into either side of the stem, forming the *Ankylosaurus* tail. Sprinkle the popping candy onto the popcorn, all over the tail, and press to adhere. Set on a prepared cookie sheet to set, 5 to 10 minutes.
4. Wrap in cellophane bags or store in an airtight container, separated with layers of parchment paper.

FIELD GUIDE:

ANKYLOSAURUS

What's the closest thing dinosaurs have to a tank? That distinction goes to *Ankylosaurus*. Its plates of thick, knobby bone, called osteoderms, embedded within its skin act as a natural armor, making it one tough adversary. In fact, *Ankylosaurus*'s hide is strong enough to withstand attacks from larger predators, including *Tyrannosaurus rex*. It originally lived almost to the very end of the Cretaceous Period, approximately sixty-six million years ago. The first specimen was discovered early in the twentieth century in northern Montana. Few other remains have been found, and a complete skeleton continues to elude fossil hunters. It can grow to a length of over thirty feet and at full size can weigh nearly eight metric tons. Visitors who choose to take a Gyrosphere tour can get a good look at *Ankylosaurus*, but don't drift too close! While it's an herbivore and not aggressive by nature, it can become agitated if it's approached or feels trapped.

--- FOOTPRINT ---

LENGTH
9.6M (31.49 ft)

HEIGHT
3.6M (11.81 ft)

HEIGHT
1.88M (6.16 ft)

WEIGHT
8 tonnes (17,600 lbs)

THREE-HORN SUNDAE

Why have a typical banana split sundae when you can have one that looks like a dinosaur? Modeled after the *Triceratops*, with their distinctive crest and horns, this sundae is pure fun for dinosaur lovers of all ages.

YIELD: 1 SUNDAE FOR TWO

3 ounces white chocolate melting wafers

1 cup heavy cream

2 bananas, frozen in the peel for 20 to 30 minutes

¼ cup chocolate chips

½ teaspoon vanilla extract

1 tablespoon sugar

3 scoops chocolate ice cream, or flavor of choice

6 to 8 ruffled cookies, such as gingersnaps or waffle cookies

SPECIAL SUPPLIES

Pastry bag and large star tip, or large resealable plastic bag

1. In a microwave-safe bowl, heat the white chocolate and 2 tablespoons of the heavy cream for 30 seconds. Remove from microwave to stir, and repeat with another 30 seconds in the microwave. Stir until smooth. Line a cookie sheet with parchment paper and set aside.

2. Remove the bananas from the freezer and peel. Cut one of the bananas in half, crosswise, creating two long horns. Cut a shorter end from the other banana to create the short horn and two thick slices to create the eyes (there will be leftover banana). Dip each horn and both eyes into the white chocolate to coat, and then place one chocolate chip in the center of each eye. Place the horns and eyes on the cookie sheet, and allow to sit for 10 to 15 minutes, or until the chocolate is set.

3. To make the whipped cream, place the remaining heavy cream, vanilla extract, and sugar in the bowl of a stand mixer with the whisk attachment and beat on high until stiff peaks form. A hand mixer would also work for this step. Place the whipped cream in a pastry bag fitted with a star tip. If you do not have a pastry bag, you can use a resealable plastic bag, and cut the corner off to dispense.

4. In a shallow bowl, arrange the 3 scoops of ice cream in an inverted triangle to create the base of the face. Pipe whipped cream along the back edge of the two upper scoops to form the base of the cookie crest. Arrange the cookies to create the crest. Press the long horns into the upper scoops, and place the eyes and the short horn directly underneath them. Pipe more whipped cream around the horns and scatter the remaining chocolate chips around the edges.

5. Serve immediately before she melts!

A VERY "BLUE" BIRTHDAY CAKE

A birthday party at Jurassic World is a very special event that includes a very special centerpiece: a cake in the shape of the dinosaur of your choosing. Here, we're including the instructions and schematics for one of the most popular versions of this fabulous cake: Blue, the alpha of our raptor pack. The recipe itself is a classic birthday cake lightly flavored with orange juice, but the presentation—which uses gumballs, jelly beans, gummy fruit and other assorted candies to form an edible portrait of Blue—is sure to make your next party an event to remember.

YIELD: 12 TO 14 SERVINGS

FOR THE CAKE BATTER:

3 eggs

1 cup whole milk

2 tablespoons orange juice

1 teaspoon vanilla bean paste or vanilla extract

2¼ cups all-purpose flour

1¼ cups sugar

4 teaspoons baking powder

¼ teaspoon kosher salt

¾ cup (1½ sticks) butter, softened

FOR THE FROSTING:

¼ cup meringue powder

⅔ cup water

12 cups sifted powdered sugar, divided

1¼ cups unsalted butter, softened, cut into tablespoon-size chunks

½ teaspoon salt

2 teaspoons vanilla extract

Food coloring

Assorted candies for decoration, such as gumballs, banana-shaped candies, grapefruit-slice gummies, jelly beans, and/or candy corn

TO MAKE THE CAKE:

1. Grease and flour the bottoms of two 8-inch cake pan, or cover them with parchment paper cut to size. Line cupcake pan with liners. Preheat the oven to 350°F.

2. Whisk the eggs in a medium bowl. Add the milk, orange juice, and vanilla. Set aside.

3. In the bowl of a stand mixer with the paddle attachment (or in a large mixing bowl using a hand mixer), combine the flour, sugar, baking powder, and salt. Mix until combined. Add the softened butter, stirring on low until a coarse crumb mixture forms.

4. Add most of the milk mixture to the flour, reserving ½ cup. Mix on medium (or high, if using the hand mixer) for about 2 minutes. Stop the mixer, add the remaining ½ cup milk, and beat for 1 minute more. Stop the mixer again, scrape down the sides of the bowl, and mix about 30 seconds more. Pour the batter into the cake pans and cupcake pan, filling each pan up only halfway. Bake cake and cupcakes for 15 to 20 minutes, or until a cake tester comes out clean.

5. Remove the cake from the oven, place on a wire rack, and let cool 15 minutes. Run an offset spatula or butter knife gently around the edge of the cake pans to loosen the cakes. Cover each cake pan with a cookie sheet, and flip over quickly to release the cake from the pan. Transfer to a wire rack until completely cool.

CONTINUED ON PAGE 113

① ② ③

SPECIAL SUPPLIES:
SPECIAL SUPPLIES:

Blue's Birthday Cake Template, page 145

Two 8-inch cake pans

Cupcake pan and liners

13-by-18-inch cake board or cutting board

Pastry bag

Offset spatula

TIP:

Use a small piece of clean bubble wrap to create the texture of Blue's scales in the icing.

TO MAKE THE FROSTING:

6. In the bowl of a stand mixer with the whisk attachment, combine the meringue powder and water. Whip at high speed until peaks form. Add 4 cups of powdered sugar, 1 cup at a time, mixing well after each addition.

7. Alternate between adding the butter pieces and the remaining sugar until it is all incorporated. It is important that your butter is softened, as it will not incorporate otherwise. Add the salt and vanilla extract, and beat on low until smooth.

8. If using immediately, let stand at room temperature. To store, transfer to an airtight container and refrigerate up to 1 week. Allow to come to room temperature before using.

9. To create the colors for Blue, reserve about a cup of frosting and dye the rest a blue-gray using a mix of blue and black. Split the reserved frosting, dying half a darker blue and leaving the rest white.

TO ASSEMBLE THE CAKE:

10. When the cakes are completely cool, find a cake board or cutting board that will fit the assembled dinosaur, at least 13 by 18 inches.

11. Cut the cakes according to the template (page 145), forming the back, head, tail, and neck of the dinosaur. Use frosting to "glue" the two back pieces together, with some frosting under the cut edges to secure in place on the cake board. Reserve all cake scraps—these will help you create haunches and forelimbs. Use the same technique to place the tail. Trimming as necessary, arrange the neck piece, two cupcakes, and the head pieces together, using frosting to secure. Transfer to the refrigerator and chill for at least 30 minutes.

12. Create a crumb coat mixture by thinning about 1 cup of the blue-gray frosting with 1 tablespoon or less of milk. Apply a light crumb coat to the entire dinosaur. Transfer to the refrigerator and chill for another 30 minutes.

13. Remove the cake from the refrigerator, and frost completely. Once frosted, working with a pastry bag and an offset spatula, use the frosting to create details and texture. Finish up with the candy accents, creating, eyes, claws, scales, and other special characteristics.

GENTLE GIANTS CHURRO FRIES

Coated with powdered sugar and paired with a salted caramel dipping sauce, these tiny churros are about the size of a crinkle fry and completely irresistible. You can find these at the park in the area around the Gentle Giants Petting Zoo, but we think you'll love them just as much when you serve them fresh and warm in your own kitchen.

YIELD: 4 TO 6 SERVINGS

FOR THE SALTED CARAMEL SAUCE:
1 cup sugar
¼ cup water
½ cup heavy cream
½ teaspoon black lava or sea salt
Juice of ½ lime

FOR THE CHURROS:
About 2 quarts of oil, for frying, such as peanut, canola, or safflower
1 cup water
½ cup unsalted butter
¼ teaspoon kosher salt
1 cup all-purpose flour
3 eggs, beaten
2 tablespoons heavy whipping cream

TO MAKE THE CARAMEL SAUCE:

1. In a large heavy-bottomed saucepan with a tight-fitting lid, carefully pour the sugar into the center of the pan. Slowly pour the water around the sugar. Turn on the heat, and adjust to medium. Use a long-handled wooden spoon to gently draw the water through the sugar to moisten completely. Do not stir. As the mixture begins to bubble, place a lid on the pot and allow it to simmer, undisturbed, for 3 minutes. After 3 minutes, check to see if the mixture is clear. If there is still a bit of cloudiness, cover and cook for 1 minute more.

2. When the mixture is clear, swirl the pot gently but do not stir, until the mixture turns a deep amber color. This could take up to 15 minutes. When the sugar has caramelized, remove from the heat and carefully add the cream (the mixture will bubble and sputter as the cream is added). Stir gently until combined. Gently stir in the salt and lime. Set aside until ready to serve.

CONTINUED ON PAGE 116

DON'T MISS

Gentle Giants Petting Zoo

While dinosaurs roam all across the island, there's only one place in Jurassic World where you can walk among and even play with them. The Gentle Giants Petting Zoo is one of the park's most popular attractions, offering unparalleled access to several of our most people-friendly animals. Young members of our *Apatosaurus*, *Gallimimus*, *Stegosaurus*, and *Triceratops* families—to name just a few—are found here each day, for visitors to interact with, pet, and feed. The zoo even offers *Triceratops* rides for small children. This controlled and totally safe environment is where these dinosaurs spend their early years before being moved to the larger habitats around the island. Visitors are advised to leave hats and small bags in our holding area before entering the zoo, as our eager young residents might try to eat them!

FOR THE CINNAMON SUGAR TOPPING:
½ cup sugar
1 tablespoon cinnamon

SPECIAL SUPPLIES:
Pastry bag and small star tip
Fry thermometer

TO MAKE THE CHURRO FRIES:

3. Add 2 quarts of oil to a large Dutch oven with a fry thermometer. Heat the oil on medium-high until it is between 350 and 365°F.

4. While the oil is coming up to temperature, make the churro batter. In a large heavy saucepan over medium-high, heat the water, butter, and salt until it reaches a rolling boil. Stir in the flour. Continue to cook, stirring continuously, until the mixture forms into a ball of dough, about 1 minute. Remove the pan from the heat, add in the eggs, and beat, with a wooden spoon, until smooth. Add the heavy whipping cream, and stir until incorporated.

5. Scoop the batter into a large pastry bag fitted with a small open star tip. When the oil has reached the correct temperature, pipe long strands of dough directly into the hot oil, using a knife or kitchen shears to cut the strand from the pastry tip. Cook only a few churros at a time—do not overcrowd the oil. Cook the churros, turning gently, until they are golden brown on all sides, about 1 minute. Briefly transfer the cooked churros to a paper towel–lined plate to drain before tossing in cinnamon sugar.

6. Serve while still warm with the caramel sauce on the side.

COMPY PACK CURLY FRIES

Here's the thing about curly fries: You know you can't eat just one. Just as their namesake, Jurassic World's *Compsognathus*, or "Compys," travel in groups, so too do our thin yet zesty sweet potato fries. And don't worry, we pack them with a heck of a lot of flavor! With dipping sauces, they make great appetizers, and they're also a perfect side for sandwiches, burgers, or our Jurassic Dog (page 49). Our version incorporates a little coconut twist for a regional flair.

YIELD: 4 SERVINGS

2 medium sweet potatoes, about 8 to 12 ounces
1 tablespoon coconut oil, melted
1 tablespoon olive oil
½ teaspoon sea salt
1 teaspoon red curry powder

SPECIAL SUPPLIES:

Spiralizer

1. Scrub and peel the sweet potatoes. Use your spiralizer set to the "thick" setting to spiralize the potatoes according to the machine's instructions. Toss the spirals in a large bowl with the oils and seasonings, and set aside.
2. Put two baking sheets in the oven and preheat to 425°F.
3. Remove the baking sheets from the oven and divide the spirals between them, spreading them out in a single layer. Bake for 10 minutes, and then rotate the spirals from the edge of the pans into the center, removing any that have already browned. Bake for another 5 to 10 minutes, watching closely, as they can burn quickly.
4. Serve immediately, sprinkled with more salt to taste.

TIP:

If you don't have a spiralizer, look for pre-spiraled sweet potatoes in the produce section.

DINO TRACKS SHORTBREAD COOKIES

Far more than simple depressions in the soil, fossilized dinosaur footprints often preserve evidence of skin patterns and other fine details about which scientists could otherwise only speculate. These sorts of fossils include information about the animal itself as well as the environment in which it may have lived. Inspired by these important fossils finds, these buttery cookies decorated with chocolate dinosaur tracks will blaze a trail right into the mouths of hungry youngsters everywhere.

YIELD: ABOUT 32 COOKIES

½ cup packed light brown sugar
¼ cup granulated sugar
1 cup (2 sticks) butter, softened
4 ounces cream cheese, softened
1 egg
1 teaspoon vanilla bean paste
3 cups all-purpose flour
¼ cup unsweetened cocoa powder
½ cup semisweet chocolate, melted

SPECIAL SUPPLIES:

Square cookie cutter
Plastic dinosaur toys
Pastry brush

1. In a stand mixer fitted with a paddle attachment, cream together the sugars, butter, and cream cheese on medium-high. Add egg and vanilla, and beat until combined. Slowly add in flour, 1 cup at time, mixing it in between each addition until a smooth dough forms. Scrape down the sides of the mixer to make sure all ingredients are incorporated.
2. Divide the dough in half, and pat each half gently into a disc. Wrap each disc in plastic wrap or parchment paper and refrigerate for at least 1 hour.
3. Line two cookie sheets with baking mats or parchment paper. Preheat the oven to 350°F.
4. Roll out the dough on a lightly floured surface roll, one disc at a time, to a ¼-inch thickness. Use your cookie cutter to cut out squares, and arrange them on the cookie sheets.
5. To make the tracks, pour the cocoa powder into a shallow dish. Walk each dinosaur toy through the cocoa powder, making sure her feet are well covered, and then press firmly into a cookie. It is okay if the cookie splits or cracks a bit. When all the cookies on a cookie sheet have been stamped, chill them in the freezer for 10 minutes.
6. Bake the cookies for 9 to 12 minutes, or until the edges are just starting to brown. Transfer immediately to a wire rack to cool.
7. Once all the cookies are baked and cooled, use a pastry brush to apply melted chocolate, diagonally, to one corner, for that "fresh from the dig" look. Place the cookies on a baking mat or parchment paper until the chocolate is set. Store in an airtight container, separated by parchment paper for 3 to 5 days.

MOUNT SIBO VOLCANIC CUPCAKES

Inspired by Mount Sibo, Isla Nublar's very own active volcano, this decadent cupcake features spiced chocolate cake and cinnamon buttercream "lava." The result is an eruption of flavor that may be too explosive for casual dessert enthusiasts to handle. Proceed with caution!

YIELD: 8 JUMBO CUPCAKES

FOR THE CAKES:
1½ cups all-purpose flour
½ cup unsweetened cocoa powder
½ teaspoon baking soda
¼ teaspoon kosher salt
½ teaspoon ground ginger
¼ teaspoon ground allspice
½ cup butter, softened
1½ cups sugar
2 eggs
¾ cup sour cream
¾ cup boiling water
2 tablespoons molasses

FOR THE CINNAMON BUTTERCREAM:
½ cup butter, softened
2 cups powdered sugar
3 tablespoons heavy cream
2 tablespoons water
1 teaspoon vanilla extract
½ teaspoon cinnamon

FOR THE CHOCOLATE GANACHE:
1⅓ cups semisweet chocolate chips
½ cup heavy cream

TO MAKE THE CAKES:

1. Preheat the oven to 350°F. Grease or line muffin pan(s) and set aside.
2. Combine the dry ingredients in a medium bowl, and whisk until well combined (there should be no lumps left from the cocoa).
3. In the bowl of a stand mixer fitted with a paddle attachment, cream together the butter and sugar on medium-high speed. Add the eggs one at a time, mixing after each addition. Scrape down the sides of the bowl, and then continue to mix until the mixture is pale yellow, light, and fluffy.
4. Add half the dry ingredients to the bowl, and mix until combined. Scrape down the sides of the bowl, add half the sour cream, and mix again. Scrape down the sides of the bowl, and repeat with the remaining dry ingredients and sour cream.
5. In a bowl or measuring cup, add the molasses to the boiling water, and stir to dissolve. With the mixer running on low, slowly add the molasses mixture to the cake mixture in a steady stream until the batter is completely combined. Fill each muffin cup full and bake for 20 to 25 minutes, or until a cake tester or toothpick comes out clean. Remove from oven and allow to cool in the pan on a wire rack for 15 minutes, and then remove the cupcakes from pan and allow to cool completely.

TO MAKE THE CINNAMON BUTTERCREAM "LAVA":

6. In a large microwave-safe bowl, beat together the butter and sugar until crumbly and well combined. In a separate small bowl, whisk together the heavy cream and water.

CONTINUED ON PAGE 122

FOR DECORATING:

24 marshmallows

Red and orange food coloring

Cookie dirt, gummy dinosaurs, candy rocks (optional)

SPECIAL SUPPLIES:

Jumbo cupcake pans and liners

TIP:

To get a nice mix of red and orange lava, place one pastry bag inside another. Fill one bag with orange buttercream and one bag with red. Cut a small hole in the tip, making sure to catch both bags.

Add the cream mixture and vanilla extract to the butter and sugar, and continue to beat until smooth. Add the cinnamon, and mix well.

7. Heat the buttercream in the microwave for 30 seconds, and mix again until smooth and the consistency of thick batter. Split in half. Add a few drops of orange food coloring to one half and a few drops of red to the other, and mix each one until you have your preferred shades of orange and red. Set aside until you're ready to assemble the cakes.

TO MAKE THE CHOCOLATE GANACHE:

8. In a medium microwave-safe bowl, combine the chocolate and the ice cream. Microwave for 1 minute, then let sit in the microwave for an additional 4 minutes. Stir until smooth. Set aside until you're ready to assemble your cakes.

TO ASSEMBLE THE CAKES:

9. When the cupcakes are completely cool, discard the liners if used and level the top of each cupcake by slicing off the dome. Turn the cakes upside down, and use a melon baller or paring knife to remove the center of each cupcake, creating a well. Be careful not to cut through to the other side. Save a "plug" of cake for each cupcake, but crumble the remaining cake scraps and reserve for plating.

10. Fill each well with buttercream, half red, half orange. Reserve the remaining buttercream for decorating. Top each well with the cake plugs and press down gently to seal. Place all the filled cupcakes, topside down, on a cooling rack placed over a silicone baking mat or parchment paper. Generously spoon ganache on top of each cupcake, allowing it to run down the sides. Use an offset spatula to smooth the ganache from the top down the sides as needed. At this point the volcanoes can be stored in the refrigerator until ready to serve, up to 24 hours if covered.

11. When ready to serve, place the marshmallows in clusters of 3 on a lined cookie sheet and toast under a broiler for 30 seconds to 1 minute. Place each volcano on a plate, use a pastry bag to add some buttercream lava, and place a marshmallow cluster on top. Sprinkle cake and cookie dirt (if using) around the volcano. Decorate with additional candies if desired.

FOSSIL DIG PUDDING

If only finding real dinosaur specimens was this easy! Put your would-be fossil hunters to work excavating this delightful treat featuring white chocolate fossilized "bones" you can create using the template in the back of the book.

YIELD: 4 SERVINGS

FOR THE PUDDING:
2 cups milk, divided
Pinch of salt
½ cup semisweet chocolate chips
3 tablespoons cornstarch
1 teaspoon vanilla bean paste, or vanilla extract

TO MAKE THE PUDDING:

1. Heat 1½ cups of the milk, salt, and chocolate chips in a heavy-bottomed saucepan over medium heat, stirring constantly, until chocolate is melted and the mixture is smooth. In a separate small bowl, mix the cornstarch with ½ cup of milk, and slowly add the mixture to the saucepan. Continue to cook on medium, stirring constantly, until the mixture begins to boil. Boil for 1 minute, then remove from heat and stir in the vanilla bean paste or vanilla extract.

2. Pour the pudding into 4 separate bowls, filling each about halfway. Cover each pudding with wax paper or plastic wrap pressed against the surface to keep a skin from forming. Allow pudding to set in the refrigerator for at least 2 hours, or overnight.

3. Pulverize the chocolate cookies in a food processor to make the "dirt" for the puddings. Store in an airtight container until ready to assemble.

CONTINUED ON PAGE 124

TO ASSEMBLE:

Four 8-ounce glass dessert cups or bowls

4 ounces chocolate wafer cookies

4 ounces white melting chocolate

½ cup heavy whipping cream

1 tablespoon powdered sugar

SPECIAL SUPPLIES:

Disposable pastry bag

Bone template

Craft paintbrush, for serving (optional)

TO MAKE THE "FOSSILS":

4. Remove the bone template (page 147) from the back of the book. Cut a piece of parchment paper to fit a cookie sheet. Lay the bone template on the cookie sheet, and then place the parchment paper over the top of it.

5. Fill the pastry bag with white melting chocolate, and close the top of the bag with a rubber band. Fill a tall glass halfway with water, and put the pastry bag inside. Microwave for 1 minute. Remove from the microwave and carefully massage the bag to help melt the chocolate. Microwave 30 seconds more if needed.

6. When the chocolate is melted and smooth, snip a small hole in the tip and pipe directly onto the parchment paper over the template to create a white chocolate "fossilized bone." Move the parchment paper, and repeat as necessary until you've created enough "bones" to decorate your puddings.

7. Slide a cookie sheet under the parchment paper and set in a cool place to set, 5 to 10 minutes, depending on thickness.

TO ASSEMBLE:

8. In the bowl of a stand mixer, fitted with a whisk attachment, whip the cream with powdered sugar until stiff peaks form. Fold in ½ cup of the cookie crumbs. Remove the pudding from the refrigerator, and layer the whipped cream on top of each dessert, followed by about a ½ inch of "dirt." Arrange 3 to 4 bones on top, and dust with more dirt.

9. Serve with a clean craft paintbrush and spoon.

DINOSAUR DOWNTOWN

Cocktails and fine dining from Jurassic World's Main Street

Even a tropical paradise teeming with dinosaurs wouldn't be complete without a few upscale dining options. Whether you're craving juicy steak and succulent scallops, or a relaxing custom cocktail after an adventurous day exploring the park, we've got you covered.

SHOWN SERVED
WITH FOSSILIZED
POTATO SPIRALS
(PAGE 130)

KING OF STEAKS

Feast your eyes on the king of steaks! This massive grilled sensation is the envy of carnivores everywhere and more than capable of satisfying even the heartiest cravings. Be sure to bring your whole appetite for this one; both its size—and its flavor—are truly awe-inspiring.

YIELD: 4 TO 6 SERVINGS

Two 1½-pound, bone-in New York strip, porterhouse, or T-bone steaks

1 teaspoon salt

Fresh ground black pepper, to taste

4 tablespoons butter, softened

1 packed tablespoon fresh thyme leaves, chopped

Pinch of red pepper flakes

1 tablespoon canola oil

Shishito peppers or red bell peppers, optional, thinly sliced

TIP:

A cast iron or stainless steel pan works best for this. Do not use a nonstick pan, as they typically aren't meant to handle the heat required.

1. A half hour before cooking, rub both sides of the steaks with the salt and pepper, and set aside to rest.

2. Make a compound butter by combining the butter, thyme, and red pepper flakes in a small bowl. Set aside.

3. Heat the oil in a large cast iron or stainless steel skillet on medium-high. Just as the oil begins to shimmer, carefully place the steaks into the skillet. Brown for 4 minutes on each side, or until a deep brown crust has formed. Do not disturb during the 4 minutes. Add the compound butter to the pan, and carefully use a spoon to baste the steaks with the butter for another 4 to 6 minutes, until the internal temperature reaches 120°F for medium rare or 125°F for medium. Transfer the steaks to a baking sheet, and tent with foil. Let rest for 10 minutes. The steaks will continue to cook during this time.

4. While the steak is resting, return the pan, with the compound butter, to medium heat and cook the peppers for 5 to 8 minutes, or until soft, stirring occasionally. Allow them to blister in some spots and baste them with the remaining butter in the pan.

5. If desired, remove the steaks from the bone and slice against the grain. Serve the meat in the pan on top of the peppers.

FOSSILIZED POTATO SPIRALS

We know potatoes have been around in one form or another since at least the time of the dinosaurs. In 2016, researchers in Patagonia discovered fossilized remains of a distant cousin to this versatile food dating back fifty-two million years. Our recipe for this popular appetizer calls for potatoes that are a bit fresher. For a hearty meal, serve this visually impressive potatoes alongside King of Steaks, page 129.

YIELD: 6 SERVINGS

6 medium (palm-size) yellow potatoes
1½ teaspoons salt
2 teaspoons paprika
¼ teaspoon cayenne pepper
4 tablespoons butter, melted
½ cup finely grated Parmesan cheese
¼ cup chopped parsley leaves

SPECIAL SUPPLIES:
6 metal skewers
Pastry brush

1. Wash and scrub the potatoes. Working in batches, place the potatoes in a microwave-safe bowl, and microwave them for 1 to 2 minutes, until slightly tender. Allow to cool.
2. Place the narrow end of the potato on a cutting board so the potato is "standing" upright. Holding it firmly, insert the skewer into the top end of the potato and all the way through, as straight as possible. Move the potato to the center of the skewer.
3. Lay the skewered potato in front of you horizontally. Using a sharp knife and starting at the narrow end, make a vertical slice into the potato, cutting all the way to the skewer at a slight diagonal angle. Hold the knife in place as you rotate the potato, pushing it toward the knife and continuing to cut downward at a shallow angle to create thin spiral slices. Repeat with all the potatoes, and set aside.
4. Place two baking sheets in the oven, and preheat both sheets and the oven to 375°F.
5. In a small bowl, combine the salt, spices, and melted butter. Gently separate the spirals of each potato, and brush them with the butter mixture, making sure to coat thoroughly. Transfer the potatoes to the hot baking sheets and bake for 15 minutes. Remove from the oven and baste with more butter, then pop them back in the oven to bake for another 30 to 40 minutes, until golden brown and crisp on the outside and fork-tender in the center. During the last 5 minutes of cooking, sprinkle the spirals with half of the Parmesan cheese.
6. Remove the spirals from the oven, slide them off the skewers onto a serving platter, and sprinkle with remaining cheese and parsley.

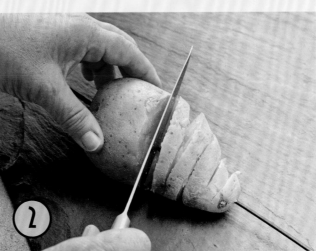

WINSTON'S SEARED SCALLOPS

Fossils of scallops and similar mollusks show they've existed in the world's oceans for more than three hundred million years. A favorite at Winston's on Main Street, these pan-seared scallops are surprisingly easy to prepare, but they look—and taste—amazing when they're done.

YIELD: 2 SERVINGS

1 pound sea scallops, or approximately 3 per serving

1 cup fresh parsley leaves

½ cup fresh basil leaves

1 tablespoon fresh thyme leaves

½ teaspoon sea salt

Juice of 1 lemon

¼ cup crème fraîche

1 teaspoon olive oil

1 tablespoon butter

3 cloves garlic, minced

½ cup dry white wine or prosecco

1. Prior to cooking, place the scallops on a plate and refrigerate for 30 minutes. Blot dry.

2. In the bowl of a food processor, combine the herbs, salt, and lemon juice, and puree until a smooth pesto-like consistency is reached, about 1 to 2 minutes. Transfer to a bowl, and whisk in the crème fraîche; set aside.

3. Heat a large skillet over medium-high heat, and brush with oil. Place the scallops in the pan, and sear on one side for 2 to 3 minutes, without disturbing. After 2 minutes, add butter and garlic, stirring to sauté. Once the butter has melted, flip the scallops, and continue to cook until just white all the way through, about 2 minutes more. Transfer the scallops to a plate, cover loosely, and set aside.

4. Add the wine to the pan and deglaze it. Cook until the liquid is reduced by half, 5 to 8 minutes. Remove the pan from the heat, add the herb mixture, and whisk until just combined.

5. Divide the sauce between two plates, and place 3 scallops on each plate. Serve immediately. This pairs well with the "Armored" Artichoke Plates (page 27) or Dinosaur Kale Salad (page 17).

MESOZOIC MARGARITA

One of the signature cocktails at the Origins Night Club on Main Street, this spicy margarita combines homemade orange-infused tequila and Serrano Orange Syrup for an after-hours drink you won't soon forget.

YIELD: 4 COCKTAILS

FOR THE INFUSED TEQUILA:

One 750-milliliter bottle of blanco (white or silver) tequila

1 large navel orange, rinsed well and cut in half

FOR THE SERRANO ORANGE SYRUP:

Peel of 1 small orange

1 large serrano pepper, cored and seeded

1 cup sugar

1 cup water

FOR THE MARGARITAS:

1 cup fresh lime juice, from 6 to 8 limes

2 cups infused tequila, recipe below

⅓ cup serrano orange syrup, recipe above

Ice

Extra limes for garnish

SPECIAL SUPPLIES:

Large bottle or jar

Skewers

Muddler

TO MAKE THE INFUSED TEQUILA:

1. Preheat the oven to 425°F.
2. Place the orange cut-side up on a baking sheet. Roast for 20 to 30 minutes, until it is blistered and caramelized. Remove from the oven and allow to cool.
3. In a container large enough to hold both the oranges and tequila, decant the tequila and submerge the oranges, using skewers to help keep them submerged. Let the tequila infuse for at least 6 hours (if infusing for longer, transfer to the refrigerator after 6 hours). Strain the tequila through a fine-mesh strainer, into a sealable container, and refrigerate until needed.

TO MAKE THE SERRANO ORANGE SYRUP:

4. Remove all the peel from the orange, leaving as much pith behind as possible. Add the orange peel, the seeded serrano pepper, sugar, and water to a small saucepan over medium-high heat, and bring to a boil, stirring, until all the sugar is dissolved, about 3 minutes. Remove from the heat and allow to cool completely, 20 to 30 minutes. Strain through a fine-mesh strainer, and refrigerate until needed.

TO MAKE THE MARGARITAS:

5. In a large pitcher mix all the ingredients except the ice, and refrigerate for at least 1 hour.
6. When ready to serve, fill the pitcher the rest of the way with ice and stir. Serve over ice with a lime wedge.

AVIAN ESCAPE

Get away from it all with this refreshing cocktail featuring our famous Agua de Aviary (page 82) and your choice of vodka or rum. Don't let the name worry you—Jurassic World security protocols ensure that nothing ever "escapes" on this island except happy visitors leaving their cares behind and immersing themselves in the wonder of the park.

YIELD: 2 COCKTAILS

1 lime, quartered
4 sprigs of mint, plus more for garnish
6 ounces vodka or white rum
1 cup Agua de Aviary (page 82)
Ice
About 8 ounces soda water for topping

1. Divide half a lime (2 quarters) and 4 mint sprigs evenly between two tall glasses. Muddle the lime and mint well with a muddler. Fill half way with ice.
2. Add a 3-ounce shot of vodka or rum to each glass. Split the Agua de Aviary between both glasses, and top with soda water.
3. Garnish with the remaining lime and mint. Stir and enjoy.

JURASSIC SUNSET

You've never seen a sunset quite like the ones on Isla Nublar, where the spectacular tropical sky paints a stunning backdrop for the graceful silhouettes of the *Apatosauruses* roaming their grassy habitats or the swooping movements of the *Pteranodons*. This layered drink is inspired by that enchanting moment at dusk when the sky changes colors and the dinosaurs start to settle for the night. It's the perfect way to end your day at the park.

YIELD: 1 COCKTAIL

2 tablespoons natural cherry syrup
Crushed ice
2 ounces grapefruit juice
2 ounces pineapple juice
3 ounces rum
1 natural bar cherry

1. Place the syrup in the bottom of a highball glass and fill with crushed ice.
2. Float the grapefruit juice over the syrup. Let rest for 1 full minute.
3. In a separate bowl or measuring cup, mix the pineapple juice and rum. Pour the pineapple and rum mixture over the back of the spoon, layering it over the grapefruit juice. Top with a cherry.
4. Serve immediately with a stir stick or straw.

AVIAN ESCAPE

MESOZOIC MARGARITA

JURASSIC SUNSET

ISLA NUBLAR FLOATING CHEESECAKES

Much like Jurassic World itself, our final recipe is an exercise in creativity in which something old is made new again. Our take on this classic dessert is inspired by Isla Nublar itself, our island paradise that serves not only as a vacation destination but also as a portal to understanding the planet we all—dinosaur and human alike—call home.

YIELD: 4 TO 6 SERVINGS

FOR THE BLUEBERRY SAUCE:
10 ounces frozen blueberries
¼ cup lime juice
½ cup sugar
Zest of 1 lime

FOR THE CHEESECAKE:
10 ounces gingersnap cookies, pulverized in a food processor
1 tablespoon sugar
5 tablespoons butter, melted
Zest of 1 lime
8 ounces cream cheese, softened
½ cup sweetened condensed milk
4 tablespoons lime juice
½ teaspoon vanilla bean past

TO MAKE THE BLUEBERRY SAUCE:

1. Combine all the ingredients except the lime zest in a medium saucepan over medium-high heat. Bring the mixture to a boil, and then reduce to a simmer and cook for 10 minutes, or until the mixture is thick enough to coat the back of a spoon. Remove from heat, add the lime zest, stir, and allow to cool.

2. Once completely cool, store in an airtight container in the refrigerator until ready to serve.

TO MAKE THE CHEESECAKE:

3. Preheat the oven to 350°F. Line a muffin tin with cupcake liners, and set aside.

4. In a large bowl, combine the gingersnap cookie crumbs with the sugar, butter, and lime zest, and mix until the mixture holds together when pressed. Place a tablespoon of crumb mixture in each cupcake liner, and press down to form a flat crust. (Extra crumb mixture can be toasted on a rimmed baking sheet for garnish.) Bake for 5 minutes, or until lightly toasted and fragrant. Set on a wire rack to cool, and then store in an airtight container until ready to use.

5. In the bowl of a stand mixer, fitted with whisk attachment, whip the cream cheese until fluffy, and then add sweetened condensed milk, lime juice, and vanilla bean paste. Whip until smooth. Pour into a shallow container with a tight-fitting lid, and refrigerate for 2 to 3 hours, until firm.

6. Spoon the blueberry sauce over the bottom of four dessert plates until completely covered. This is your "ocean." Gently remove the crusts from the cupcake liners and place three on each plate. Using an ice cream scoop, scoop cheesecake mixture onto each "island" of crust. Sprinkle with additional crumb mixture, and serve immediately.

MEASUREMENT CONVERSION CHARTS

VOLUME

CUP	OZ	TBSP	TSP	ML
1	8	16	48	240
3/4	6	12	36	180
2/3	5	11	32	160
1/2	4	8	24	120
1/3	3	5	16	80
1/4	2	4	12	60

TEMPERATURES

°F	°C
200°	93.3°
250°	120°
275°	135°
300°	150°
325°	165°
350°	177°

WEIGHT

US	METRIC
0.5 OZ	14 G
1 OZ	28 G
¼ LB	113 G
⅓ LB	151 G
½ LB	227 G
1 LB	454 G

ABOUT THE AUTHORS

Dayton Ward is a *New York Times* best-selling author or co-author of more than 40 novels and novellas. His short fiction has appeared in more than 25 anthologies, and he has written for publications such as *NCO Journal, Kansas City Voices, Famous Monsters of Filmland, Star Trek Magazine,* and *Star Trek Communicator* as well as the websites Tor.com, StarTrek.com, and Syfy.com. He lives in Kansas City with his wife and two daughters, and you can find him on the web at http://www.daytonward.com.

Elena Pons Craig is a food and prop stylist and recipe developer with more than twenty-five years of experience in culinary design, marketing, photography, and publishing. She has a deep love for pop culture and for using it to have fun with food. She lives with her family in Fairfax, California.

INSIGHT
EDITIONS

PO Box 3088
San Rafael, CA 94912
www.insighteditions.com

Find us on Facebook: www.facebook.com/InsightEditions
Follow us on Twitter: @insighteditions

Library of Congress Cataloging-in-Publication Data available.

ISBN: 978-1-64722-106-5

Publisher: Raoul Goff
VP of Licensing and Partnerships: Vanessa Lopez
VP of Creative: Chrissy Kwasnik
VP of Manufacturing: Alix Nicholaeff
Editorial Director: Vicki Jaeger
Designers: Judy Wiatrek Trum and Lola Villanueva
Editor: Hilary VandenBroek
Editorial Assistant: Anna Wostenberg
Senior Production Editor: Jennifer Bentham
Production Manager: Sam Taylor
Production Associate: Deena Hashem
Senior Production Manager: Greg Steffen
Senior Production Manager, Subsidiary Rights: Lina s Palma

Photographer: Ted Thomas
Food and Prop Stylist: Elena P. Craig

Insight Editions, in association with Roots of Peace, will plant two trees for each tree used in the manufacturing of this book. Roots of Peace is an internationally renowned humanitarian organization dedicated to eradicating land mines worldwide and converting war-torn lands into productive farms and wildlife habitats. Roots of Peace will plant two million fruit and nut trees in Afghanistan and provide farmers there with the skills and support necessary for sustainable land use.

Manufactured in China by Insight Editions

10 9 8 7 6 5 4 3 2 1

BIRTHDAY CAKE TEMPLATE

WHAT YOU NEED:

2 x 8" Cake layers
2 cupcakes

1. Lay the two halves flat side down in the center of the cake board.
2. Arrange the tail and neck on the cake board as desired.
3. Use the cupcakes to add details to the head to better define eye sockets and place the cake pieces for the head in front of the cupcakes for the snout. Cut to preference.

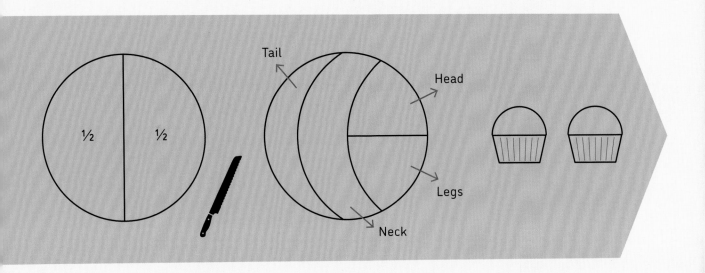

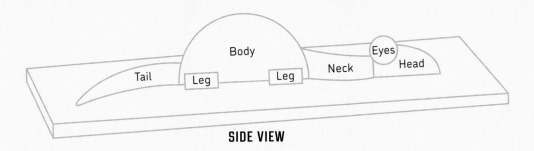

SIDE VIEW

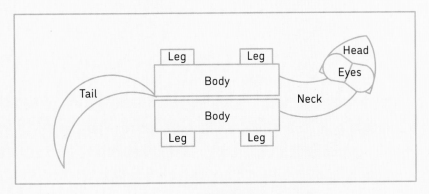

TOP VIEW

FOSSIL DIG PUDDING TEMPLATE